COSMOS THEOLOGY

The Meaning of Pantheism and its Application to an Emergent World Order

JANUS

Library and Archives Canada Cataloguing in Publication

CIP data on file with the National Library and Archives

ISBN 978-1-55483-911-7

The Tree of Knowing Good and Evil

"…do not eat from the tree of knowing good and evil;…" (Genesis 2:17). The Tree of Knowing Good and Evil symbolizes the enlightenment of *Cosmos Theology*. Knowledge has always been a threat to the myth religions, and there is no surprise that the fear of it is inscribed into the Bible. The original context of that tree is evil, being the tree that produced the apple eaten by Eve, but how telling of the Christian religion to associate evil with knowledge! And that same fear of knowledge has been transmitted down through the centuries by institutionalized religions. Galileo was put under house arrest and Giordano Bruno was burned alive for his intuition about stars. Knowledge of evolution is fundamental to modern medicine yet churches have opposed it since the days of Darwin. Not only Christianity, though, has taught that humanity is unworthy of enlightenment. The Greek Prometheus was chained to a mountain by Zeus for his gift of fire to humanity that enabled progress and civilization. The time is upon us when humanity can break the chains imposed by mythical gods. Let us eat heartily from the Tree of Knowing Good and Evil. This essay is the beginning.

I

With most aspects of our lives when we wish to know whether a particular idea, belief or manner of thinking is correct we generally take the trouble to search out factual support. If the belief cannot be verified directly by our senses, for example the atomic structure of matter, people have not been content to merely wallow in speculation and have undertaken ingenious tests of their hypotheses. The rational method has been exceptionally beneficial, although faith healers can still claim evil spirits to be the cause of insanity and sickness, as the evidence of chemical imbalance and germs is largely circumstantial.

Given the vast benefits of the reasoning mind, which everyone acknowledges from daily experience, the wonder is that any other manner of thought could explain the more fundamental nature of our being, yet traditionally metaphysical explanations of Creation, good and evil, morality and natural phenomena continue to be believed by the vast majority of mankind. Among people who have lost traditional faith, ethics and morality have become relative, based on the needs of human beings in varying circumstances. Where the old metaphysical reasons for behavior are discredited the humanization of ethics can be expected, for is not correct behavior meant to benefit people in the first place? We may heartily agree that it is, except when human behavior is justified by 'happiness' we must first decide if the causes of 'happiness' are always moral. That people can live both happy and immoral lives appears evident, and the act of the martyr suffering for humanity challenges the modern philosophy: "If it is right for you, do it."

Described here are the precepts of pantheism, the religion that equates *God* to the laws and forces of the Universe. Because of its reliance on science and reason the atheist might refer to pantheism as disguised atheism, but this assessment would not be accurate. Pantheists believe in a Higher Power to the Universe, only one that is manifested as a destiny without being metaphysical. That Higher Power is of the Universe itself. One might say *Nature.* The difference from our common understanding of Nature is that the term usually applies only to our immediate biological world. The pantheist position is to apply Nature to the farthest stars. Pantheism (better named *Cosmostheism*) is therefore a natural evolution of religious thought. The pagans of ancient Rome also thought of Christians as "atheists," since they had no immediate gods before them that could give comfort and solace from their bedrooms and pantries, but instead reduced many gods to one single, unseen God. This must indeed have seemed an emotional let down. To accuse Christians today of being atheists would be ludicrous, and the same will be seen true of Cosmos believers in the future. We came from somewhere and our existence has meaning. This is a religious assertion, not an atheistic one, with the difference from traditional religion being its derivation from rational contemplation instead of mystical supposition. The elements of our bodies compose in a particular way to make us. We are conceived and born. It is Nature. Those same elements were forged in stars billions of years ago. That too is Nature – the Universe as Creator. Is there not an awesome aspect to this knowledge? Why, then, do we need anything mystical for a religion? That is what every pantheist asks.

In this question is *not* meant to imply that people who

have had 'near-death experiences' are delusional, or have not had 'spiritual' occurrences that were meaningful in their lives. Many people have had their lives significantly altered by those experiences. Even with the science of today we can still only claim to have the dimmest understanding of underlying reality. The quantum world is totally bizarre by the standards of our macro existence, and no one can claim absolute certainty, whether pro or con, on human existence beyond death. The only absolute truth about 'life after death' is that we *do not know.* Those who would say they do, perhaps having had 'near-death experiences' themselves, should realize that having survived those experiences they *remember* them. That means their brains were functioning. A dead brain cannot remember. Therefore, we have to remain skeptical on whether the people with those experiences were actually dead. There is also evidence that the same experiences are caused by abnormal functioning of dopamine and oxygen flow in research subjects who are very much alive.

The purpose of this writing is to present the precepts of a rational religion derived from Nature and to discern the political consequences of that religion. In the process it will be demonstrated that in matters that have fallen within the field of traditional religion there is no need to extend beyond this Universe we know; show that the relativistic, liberal and humanistic outlook cannot only be false, it can be destructive; and present a rational basis for ethical behavior derived from simple observation, deduction and natural laws. All that is asked of the reader is recognition that our only means of *proving* anything is through reason based on observation, or by extrapolations of the probable, and therefore we should suspect imagined experiences impressed on the emotions as revelations of 'truth'. We live in a natural Universe, with natural causes either for good or evil that require no supernatural explanation, and as inhabitants of this Universe our common sense should tell us we are duty bound to believe only what is within our realm of experience. The tragedy of traditional belief is that by natural selection of belief systems over millennia the absolutes required for human society have been established: "Thou shalt not murder, Thou shalt not steal," etc., while continuing to implement those absolutes on a supernatural causality. When this supernatural causality is undermined in an enlightened era the absolutes are unpinned. Here the problem of absolutes is solved without traditional religion.

II

In the Beginning there were no atoms or even atomic particles. All were as one, fused into a fireball trillions of degrees in temperature. In those first moments space itself expanded, at a speed faster than light. The spreading plasma cooled and out of it coalesced the simplest atoms, of hydrogen and helium. Thus the Universe was born. From that Beginning the Universe has continued its expansion, in four dimensions, three of space and one of time. Like dots on an expanding balloon, galaxies of stars continue their motion away from each other, and just as the surface of a balloon has no edge or center, neither does the Universe.

The first stars fused their hydrogen and helium atoms into heavier elements, and after burning for millions of years exploded to give still heavier elements. Clouds of dust and gas then littered the galaxies to condense once again into new stars, only this time there was more than hydrogen and helium. Planets also formed from the debris of former stars and the miracle of life could emerge. In such manner life is made of star-stuff, 13.8 billion years after the Beginning.

The Universe encompasses all that exists. There is nothing outside the Universe, for if there were it would be included in the Universe. Therefore nothing leaves the Universe nor enters it, and all forces of Creation are *within* it. Let us dispel all notions of mystical creation from force or forces that are *above* Nature, i.e., *super*natural. Hard science gives confirmation to a lack of metaphysical cause, for when we look into matter at the atomic level we find no certainty, only probability, even in principle. To have certainty we must have higher levels of mass,[1] so that at our human level we can make predictions with precision knowing Newton's equations. If spiritual existence and mass are incompatible, and it is mass that gives certainty, there can be no role for metaphysical presence in a material Universe. Consequently, the only way to understand the Universe is by rational contemplation using fact, empiricism and logic, and we must realize that mysticism, with its supposition of knowledge, short-circuits genuine understanding.

Since the Beginning Creation has continued and was not a single event in time. Creation is on going; it has never stopped, meaning the development of order into increasing complexity. A religion derived from the Universe should tell us something about a dynamic Universe, because only then can we know anything about human destiny and the laws that should govern human behavior. *Complexity Theory*, the study of how parts interact in a system, is giving us an idea of cosmogenesis, but first let us assure ourselves that order is real and not subjective. This might seem obvious, although any arrangement could be declared equal to any other. Definitions of order have been varied and contentious, including one that order is anything we want it to be. Here we take the common view that order is a state brought into existence by the expenditure of energy, without which its existence would be improbable. To draw cards in order from a randomly shuffled deck, although possible is improbable, requiring effort and training to accomplish for a magic show. An explosion,

---

1 From physics, $w = h/p$ where w is the length of a 'matter wave,' h is Planck's constant and p is momentum. A smaller w means more certainty of position, given by a higher p, i.e., more mass. We know with certainty where a stone is located but not an electron. The equation is relevant on the atomic scale.

on the other hand, also expends energy, but its scattered results are probable, not improbable.

We can therefore think of order as being representative of
energy, so that higher order represents more energy than
lower order. A constructed building certainly has more order
than a pile of lumber lying on the ground. Workers have to
expend energy to put that lumber into the more ordered construction, so besides increased order a building also represents
a higher energy state than a pile of lumber. The same is true
of many examples in Nature, not just those created by human
beings. Sugar is a complex molecule made in plants by using
sunlight, and is broken down by animals to retrieve that energy. Nuclei of atoms have a positive electric charge that must
be overcome by added protons to build heavier elements. The
larger nuclei then have more energy that can be released by
fission in atomic power plants. That build-up of nuclei is ac-
complished in the hot interiors of stars, by such large numbers
of protons moving so rapidly that the improbability of building heavy elements becomes a probability. From many examples we see that order is an improbable state that requires
energy to obtain, and its material realization is representative
of an energy status.

Physicists will object to this understanding of order, because order is also formed from the simple loss of energy.
Cold, solid ice certainly has more order than boiling liquid
water, so that in cases like this higher order represents *less*
energy than lower order. Systems can form that represent
less energy than the sum of the energy of their individual
components. The building of atomic nuclei, mentioned
above, is accompanied by the *release* of energy when the ki-
netic motion of protons combined with the nuclear force is
sufficient to overcome the repulsive positive charge on nuclei, leaving assemblies with less total energy than the sum

of the original particles. In the house analogy, the energy of workers needed in its construction can be partially offset by less man-hours for the construction of an equally functional apartment, so we are not surprised to see in large metropolitan areas the construction of large apartment buildings, although the major reason is the cost of land. Similarly, higher social development is made possible by economic integration of workers whose expertise in narrow fields replaces the generalized knowledge of less specialized workers. In a hypothetical context, if present day nations could scrap their armies under a united world order, the resulting unity would be a more efficient, less wasteful order than our present world of sovereign nations with many armies. But the world would still need a military to maintain that UWO. It is in this sense that we can think of order even in systems that have undergone self-organization as representing energy. It is just more efficient order.

Examples of order and its forces in Nature are legion. Atoms and molecules are held together by the interaction of repulsive and attractive electrical and nuclear forces. The Solar System is an ordered arrangement between gravitation and inertia, as are the galaxies. The evolution of life into higher forms is torturous, made possible by natural selection where only the fittest survive and all else is exterminated. To bring common elements together and form a new organic cell would be an impossibility ranging in the billions to one if there were no guiding forces involved. The birth of a baby requires discomfort and effort on the part of the mother, and its proper rearing as a child requires much care. It is evident that in the fields of human endeavor, whether manufacture, social progress, thought or art,[2] anything man made is always ac-

2 This notion of effort in artistic creation considers the time spent by the master in perfecting his/her talent.

complished only after a struggle, by people who were willing to accept the respective challenges. All of these are examples of ordered states and their energy requirements.

We are accustomed to religion announcing the authority of its godhead and from that authority all Creation is performed. Pantheism is disadvantaged as a religion because the authority of Nature is natural and therefore may not seem to be an authority at all, thereby detracting from it as any motivation for religious belief. The usual reaction of the human mind when contemplating order is to conclude that forethought was required for its occurrence. People make things, and therefore when we see order we believe forethought must have brought it into existence. The fallacy of that conclusion can be seen from trial-and-error, which we know can bring new and improved developments yet occurs under the condition of ignorance. Some changes work but most do not because the choices made are always guesses, and the same in Nature where trial-and-error is always *blind*. Because Nature is blind the pantheist must prove its authority from science to show how changes that work survive and go on to produce more changes, some that succeed but the majority probably not. Natural creation can be understood from the repetition of simple occurrences, especially when large numbers are involved over lengthy periods of time, so that the Universe itself can be considered the *Creator* of all things. The resulting complexity can seem miraculous, but by removing the mystical pantheism merely removes the authority of a godhead. Since notions on Creation are a major difference from our usual understanding of religion, let us see how natural order occurs that justifies the claim of the Universe as *Creator:*

A familiar example of self-organization is an economy. A free economy has no directorate, yet from millions of people working, buying and selling anonymously, each pursuing his or her own interests, a country sustains itself and even progresses. Lack of real understanding about markets is shown when they crash. When attempts are made to control an economy, as was done in the Soviet Union, it stagnates. The same when markets are monopolized. Cities and nations are likewise examples of self-organization, where individuals, following their own particular interests, develop complex societies. From these examples an important principle is revealed about self-organization, and that is the autonomy of its participants, yet any one is integral to the whole without being essential to it. Such systems are like a very large orchestra where musicians know their parts so well there is no need for a conductor.

Flocks of birds can dart and dash as a single organism, yet have no leader directing the flock. The same is seen with shoals of fish underwater. How could such order arise naturally without intelligent leadership? A computer simulation of the phenomenon was made in 1986 and subsequently used in movies of bats and birds. Discovered was that such complex flocking behavior is possible if each individual bird or fish follows three simple rules: 1) avoids crowding with its closest neighbors, 2) steers toward the average heading of its neighbors, 3) maintains cohesion with its neighbors. At sufficiently high density these simple rules give an overall action as if the flocks or shoals were collectively cognizant.

An example of self-organization, at first not believed by Europeans, is the synchronized flashing of fireflies in the jungles of South East Asia. For kilometers along a river millions of these insects flash at the same time. How could that coordination develop spontaneously, each night? Intelligence higher than that of insects might seem to be involved, but the flashing begins with some insects that are close in synch

with each other by chance forming pockets of synchroniza-
tion within the chaos. Then others, whose flashing in the beginning was less close in frequency, adapt to the frequency
of the groups, which then adapt their frequencies to that of
the largest group until a riverside is alight in synchronicity.

The order within colonies of social insects, whether ants
or bees, has long fascinated biologists. Yet each ant or bee
follows its own individual programming, molded over millions of years, without external direction. Slime mold
demonstrates embracing order over individuals even more
remarkably, as it is a transition between single cell and multi-
cell organisms. As single cells the amoeba-like organisms
live on rotting vegetation in forests, reproducing by simple
division. When food becomes scarce the 'amoebae' move together and form their numbers into a slug, that is, into a single organism. As cells of the slug, each plays a role in service
of the whole. The slug moves in search for food, stops and
erects a stalk into the air with a spore cap. The cap bursts
and slime mold spores spread across the forest floor, each
which develops into a new individual 'amoeba' for another
cycle. Although each 'amoeba' lives as an individual, each
has potential to be part of a collective existing as a single, integrated entity.

A major goal in biology is to understand the origin of life
from inorganic chemicals. No one understands how life
began but as with the self-organization of the above examples
no spiritual notions need to be invoked. One idea on the origin of life is based on our knowledge that organic chemicals
existed on the early Earth, formed from lightening discharges
in the atmosphere of that time, in deep-sea hydrothermal
vents, or coming from space, most likely the latter. A large
variety of these organic chemicals accumulated, some interacting with each other but most probably not. Those that in-

teracted formed larger and more complex molecules. With increasing reactions the system became autocatalytic, that is, some of the assembled chemicals acted as catalysts that greatly facilitated the formation of other such molecules. Each would be both ingredient and product of reaction, but also a catalyst for another reaction, the same as enzymes.

A laboratory re-enactment of how life began may have already been achieved, at the Scripps Research Institute, 2009. RNA copies genetic information from a cell's DNA to build proteins, and can function as both gene and enzyme which has led to speculation of it being the ancestral molecule of life in a once existing RNA world. Researchers synthesized a large population of RNA enzymes and performed a test-tube evolution procedure to obtain variants most adept at joining together. Mutations occurred, resulting in the most efficient replications growing in number to dominate the mixture. The improved enzyme was capable of perpetual replication. Although not alive it was able to perform an essential function of life.

Phase transitions are sudden transformations that occur after a trend, such as water turning into ice after a period of cooling. The same happens in economies when innovations accumulate and there is an Industrial Revolution, or a complete re-organization from the invention of the automobile. The same would have happened on the early Earth as RNA molecules increased in number and efficiency. A phase transition occurred a billion years after the Earth's crust solidified sufficiently to allow cellular life, after which natural selection and lateral gene transference favored the most efficient cells in their use of elements from the environment. That continued for three billion years until the Ediacaran Period, that occurred 630 to 542 million years ago when single cells self-organized into multi-celled plants and animals in another phase transition, followed by the Cambrian "explosion" that saw the vast diversification of life.

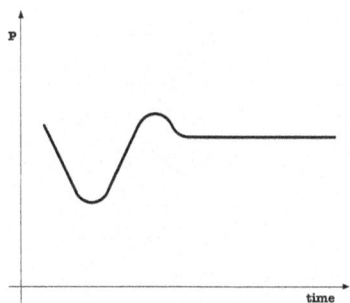 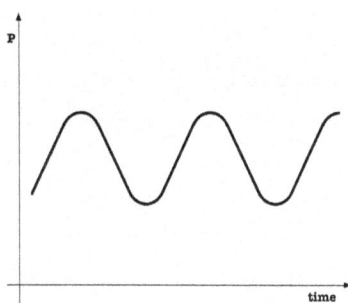

Figure 1   **Figure 2**

Order exists in time as well as materially. Systems that iterate on themselves in positive feedback exhibit a wide variety of behavior from order to chaos, a phenomenon not discovered until the invention of computers that are excellent at doing simple but tedious operations repeatedly. Populations of most animal species fluctuate, depending on predation, climate and disease. If the birthrate is very low the population quickly goes to extinction. If the birthrate is a bit higher the population first plummets but then recuperates to a steady state, shown in Figure 1. If still a bit higher Figure 2 shows the boom and bust cycle normally associated with animal populations when preyed upon. In the case of a rabbit population preyed on by foxes, its number first increases, providing more food for foxes whose number increases. With more foxes more rabbits are eaten, diminishing their number, only then the foxes have less food and their number diminishes, allowing the rabbit population to increase again, etc. As in the previous case we have an example of temporal order that could continue forever.

When the birthrate is much larger than shown for Figure

2 no prediction is possible. The graph becomes chaotic. Most intriguing is what occurs when the birthrate is not quite sufficient for that to happen. This is known as the *edge of chaos,* the very thin region where, by analogy, smooth flowing water starts to become turbulent. It is the region in animal species where evolution occurs. When in an ordered, predictable state there is too much rigidity for advancement, and in a chaotic state too much variation occurs for stabilization. The edge of chaos[3] provides both small but sufficient stability and variation. Figure 3 is shown for a birthrate giving a population whose growth is neither predictable nor chaotic.

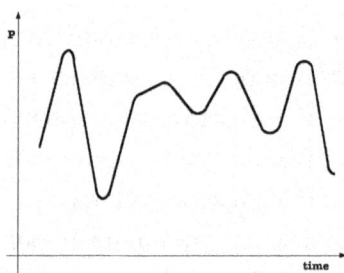

Figure 3

Several knowledgeable arguments have been advanced to disprove natural evolution, one being "irreducible complexity" proposed by biochemistry professor Michael Behe, defined as the condition of a single system when composed of several interacting parts, the removal of any one causing the system to stop functioning. The implication is that any part that is not complete or fully evolved would not allow survival of the life possessing it, therefore inferring design.

---

3 Researchers in Complexity Theory make a distinction between chaos and disorder. Chaos occurs when a small change in starting conditions causes a big change in result.

An example is the mammalian eye, which is composed of several parts, all of which must function for the animal to see. The argument can be refuted by considering the evolutionary lineage of the eye, beginning from photoreceptor cells that could detect light but not its direction. When by random mutation photoreceptor cells developed in a small skin depression, a process ensued whereby deeper depressions collimated light onto a specific group of receptors to make a pinhole camera that could discern shapes, and that is still the eye of the present day nautilus. Subsequent mutations and the selection process evolved a lens from a layer of transparent cells, and so on in an unambiguous chain of developments from a simple structure. The present mammalian eye did not appear fully developed in a one-step process, nor had to, and that evolution was not perfect. Instead of photoreceptor cells placed on the outside of the retina, where any sensible designer would attach them, light has to first pass through the retina with its cells and nerve fibers that degrade image quality.

Another argument used by Creationists to discredit natural evolution is to point out the appropriateness of animal characteristics for their environments, indicating design, forgetting that if animals were not adapted to their environments they would not be there. Following Darwin's argument, sufficiently large populations possess a variety of characteristics for any particular trait, so with a change in the environment natural selection 'weeds out' the less favorable characteristics of the animals attempting to cope with the change. Over time genetic adaptation occurs. But exactly how does this happen, considering that new mutations may be required and mutations are usually freakish, not beneficial? How do animals genetically adapt, considering the low probability of advantageous mutations that might enhance survival among very many mutations that are inconsequential or harmful?

To illustrate how adaptation occurs, let us suppose a population of deer with short legs, making them easy prey for wolves. The probability of a mutation endowing the deer with longer legs and faster escape we further suppose is one in a million, and for the purpose of argument each generation born has 100 *random* mutations. Unfortunate individuals born with any disadvantage will not last long in the wild, and those genes will be eliminated, but most mutations need not be assumed life threatening. One million mutations, assuming 100 mutations per generation, will require 10,000 generations, and if a deer generation is five years that one beneficial mutation might take 50,000 years, but Nature has lots of time. That fortunate individual born having longer legs will be less prone to being caught by wolves and over its lifetime will leave more offspring than usual for the short leg variety. Any advantageous mutation can spread rapidly throughout a population, since in this case the deer carrying it will replace the short leg deer killed by wolves. The short leg variety for reason of death will leave fewer offspring per generation than the long leg variety. Eventually by such natural selection with its different survival rate all the deer will have longer legs. The species will have evolved that feature. The fossil record confirms it. With that constant pressure extended over 30 million years we see adaptation changes in the deer family from when it was the size of sheep.

Longer legs is not the only change occurring with the passage of time, so that a deer population separated by a mountain range or simply distance will acquire other mutations different from the parent population. If the two deer populations never mix, one may acquire so many different characteristics that it will become more like moose. This in fact happened when moose first appeared in the fossil record two million years ago, making it a relatively young species. Another split-off population from the deer family became caribou, which is a species especially adapted to cold. That adaptation in the caribou case was a special fur that is hollow, making it an excellent insulator. Instead of wolves being the selector for long legs, cold was the selector in the case of caribou fur, but the process of selection acted the same. The result was an animal that the Creationist can point to as 'designed' for cold, which is correct only if we anthropomorphize the 'designer' as Nature. By imparting intelligence behind Nature the Creationist can claim a supernatural cause acting with forethought, and many religious evolutionists make that assumption in their notion that evolution could be directed, but this is a superfluous argument since without intelligence adaptation would still occur. By Occam's Razor[4] genetic adaptation is purely natural from understandable causes. As was emphasized with the deer population, *all* the mutations were purely *random*, with the only beneficial one picked from the million by uncaring natural selection. Creation *can* result from *blind* trial-and-error. This understanding was Darwin's great achievement.

From examples like the iteration explaining the rise and fall of rabbit populations we see that what appears complex in Nature starts from simple, positive feedback rules endlessly repeated. Mutations build over the millennia, honed for survival by natural selection. If life does not stick in an orderly cycle (Figures 1 and 2) the results can be surprisingly complex. The entire Universe is built by the inevitable play of such natural rules in a league that plays by all rules. The DNA of life is often referred to as a blueprint, which if the

4 One should not increase, beyond what is necessary, the number of entities required to explain anything.

analogy were true DNA would have to spell out step-by-step how every cell and organ is constructed. Instead, DNA is more like a recipe containing a few simple, repeated instructions. Flipping a coin and repeatedly marking a point according to a rule, such as how much to move north or east, for heads and another for tails, measured from a starting point, does not produce a random field of dots but a shape that becomes more defined as this "chaos game" continues. One such set of rules makes a fern pattern, so it is not surprising that some plants grow into ferns[5].

Complexity occurs at the interface, the boundary, where the forces of order meet chaos. An almost microscopic crystal of water is an orderly arrangement of atoms, that when tumbling through the atmosphere encounters multiple, unpredictable combinations of temperature, humidity and impurities. By accreting to itself atmospheric moisture under chaotic circumstances the crystal grows into the beauty of a snowflake. Evolution is caused by changes in the environment, sometimes catastrophic ones, that are unpredictable and chaotic. Mutations, that give new characteristics, are completely random. To evolve, in addition to these adaptive disruptions life must experience natural selection, which is a force tending toward stable adaptation. A balance between disturbance and stability is required.

From such examples and many more we learn that for Creation in Nature we need invent no supernatural cause. We see the same simple occurrences repeated endlessly in systems that are stable for long periods, then eventually break down and lead to new forms from what has been termed "self-organized criticality". This has been described as similar to a sand pile that has sand added to it one grain at a time. For a while nothing happens until suddenly there

5 James Gleick, *Chaos*, pages 237 -239

is an avalanche. The same is found applicable to earthquakes, traffic jams and economic collapses. More remarkably, the brain is also found to work on the same principle. Networks of brain cells alternate between periods of calm and periods of instability. Although much of the time the brain runs in a stable way, it can unpredictably lurch into a flurry of activity when a single neuron triggers a cascade of activity that propagates across small networks of brain cells, and we have a sudden epiphany out of nowhere. Neural networks in the brain have been mapped and discovered to form the right architecture for self-organized criticality. A regular network would have each node connected to its nearest neighbors, and a random network would have no regular structure, with many long-distance connections. The brain is organized between both types of architecture, with the average number of connections adapted for the brain to be on the tipping point between order and chaos. A healthy brain is balanced between the two, and does not function purely on logical operations as does a computer.

In our daily lives, of course, these rules of natural creation cannot apply because we have no control over the forces of chaos, or they would not be chaotic, only our response to them, so in human terms emphasis on the chaos side of Creation, although conducive to our enlightenment, is of little *practical* concern. For our daily lives it is the ordering side of Creation that must be emphasized, because regardless of all the examples of self-organization we can give, we know from common experience that they do not give a full description of Nature.

If we take a glass of clear, still water and slowly insert a droplet of ink into its center with an eyedropper, the ink initially hangs as a globule of color with a few streaks of tint slowly spreading outward. The initial stage is one of concentration that needs for its appearance an outside agent, namely the person who deposits the ink. In time the globule will disappear because the ink will disperse evenly throughout the water, leaving a completed mixture in the glass. This end state needs no outside agent; it is the result of random action between the molecules of ink and water and is inevitable. The resulting mixture is an illustration of what we see occurring repeatedly in Nature: the trend toward dispersion, dissipation and randomization in time. Other examples are equally evident: a house becomes untidy because that is its more probable state without a diligent housekeeper, and when a porcelain plate breaks its pieces are testimony that nothing we see or touch today will perpetually be as we know it, given sufficient time. A fence left to the random forces of wind and rain will eventually weather, and a machine without care will inevitably break down. Encompassed under one postulate, "Murphy's Law" has best given this natural trend expression: "If something can go wrong, it will." This is purely a law of probability since with inevitable change in time there are an infinite number of states to enter, where the number of higher states is limited and therefore less likely entered unless directed.

Closely related to random change in time is a fundamental law of physics, the second law of thermodynamics: the law of *entropy* that tells us in time the *utility* of energy inevitably decreases. Nothing is more fundamental than the inexorable tendency of a high-energy state to change to a state of lower energy. The most common experience we have of this is a hot object cooling. That energy can never be used again. When a pot of hot water cools its energy cannot be reused, not that it is destroyed, that energy still exists, only it exists in equilibrium with the temperature of the kitchen where it is placed. It is the *imbalance* of energy that makes it useful. There is nothing mysterious about energy dissipation; it is just another manifestation of the logic in Nature for everything to take the path of least resistance and to continue until equilibrium is reached. The *controlled* flow of energy to lower states is how we make use of energy, such as the steam in a boiler to move a machine, or the discharge of a battery. Entropy, the disutility of energy, is always increasing everywhere, whether in our kitchens or on the grand scale of the Universe. Stars are pouring out their energy into the cold of space. Eventually they will grow dark, their hydrogen fuel will be gone, space will be a little warmer and the Universe will be dead.

Because material order requires energy to build, when that order is destroyed we can think of the resulting disorder as a loss of that energy and an increase in entropy (although entropy itself should not be thought a measure of disorder, as often happens). When change is inevitable in time and the resulting state is less ordered than the initial state we can therefore name this occurrence: *entropic regression.* If entropic regression is most probable with random change, we might ask how self-organized states are possible. They originate and exist because in all cases they are *open* systems, meaning that energy and materials flow through them; they are not *closed* to the environment beyond their systems. For that reason life needs to breathe, eat and excrete. Entropy is the condition of closed systems. A room that is perfectly insulated would have its internal temperature equalize throughout. Entropy would maximize. If there were glass windows in the room that allowed heat within it to be lost to a cold exterior, the room would then be an open system. Moisture in its air would condense on the windows to form intricate patterns, giving rise in northern climates to the children's legend of "Jack Frost" who supposedly paints them. A picture of ferns and leaves in frost on the windows would result, equal to any an artist could paint and thereby suggesting the frosty creator. The most perfectly closed system of all is the Universe when considered in whole. Nothing enters or leaves the Universe and for that reason entropy prevails.

Creation is an unusual event that happens because the Universe is BIG. If there is one asset the Universe has it is *large numbers.* Everyone is aware that winning a lottery is most unlikely for one person, yet people *do* win. That is because over the full range of players chances increase with the more combinations played. It is the same in the game of life where the Universe plays *all* combinations. The improbable becomes probable. Inevitably sometime someplace conditions for life will exist no matter how unlikely for any one world. When all the conditions required by one planet to have intelligent life become known – to have water and be in the "Goldilocks" temperature zone from its sun for that water to be liquid, to rotate for moderate hours of night and day, to have a not too eccentric orbit, to have a magnetic field for protection of its atmosphere, to have tectonic plates for renewal of its surface minerals, to have an axial tilt for seasons, and undoubtedly many more features of planet Earth that make intelligent life possible – the Creationist, it seems, has reason for belief that the Earth was contrived for intelligent life. This belief becomes less certain when considering the number of planets in just our galaxy. A type of star that is particularly numerous, accounting for about 80 percent or 80 billion stars of the galaxy's 100 billion, are red dwarfs that are faint and cool compared to the Sun but long-lived, giving more opportunity for life to arise on a planet around them. It is estimated that 41 percent of all red dwarfs have a large Earth-like planet orbiting in their habitable zone where liquid water can exist. That gives 32.8 billion planets, or 32.8

billion chances. This is how the Universe works – by chance but chance bought with large numbers. No mystical spirituality is needed to explain the uniqueness of one planet for life. That includes planet Earth.

Given sufficient chance entropy *can* be reversed, only in very localized regions of space and time while their systems are *en route* to equilibrium. An analogy is a ball rolling down a hill. As it rolls its energy of height lessens but on the hill by chance there is a short hump that the ball climbs and its loss of energy is temporarily reversed. The energy of height that the ball gains on climbing the hump is the energy lost from rolling down the major part of the hill. Such is the Earth in the energy system of the Sun. To believe from the appearance of life that entropy can be denied would not be correct, because *scale* in space and time is necessary for our understanding of Creation. We can think of a weather pattern that over all is circular and its winds are in all directions, but at a particular, localized time and place the wind is felt coming from only one direction. A freezer extracts heat from its interior by the expansion of a gas, the coolant, and in this separation of heat and cold might be thought a contradiction of universal entropy, which predicts the balance of heat and cold. Entropy is indeed denied *on the scale of the freezer,* but not on the scale of the kitchen where it is placed, because on that larger scale must be included the heat of coolant compression generated and lost to the room as well as the heat of the motor. On that larger scale entropy is not denied. Creationists have offered the second law of thermodynamics as proof against evolution, since the natural construction of order manifested by life is a denial of entropic regression, but that is true only on the space-time scale of the Earth, not on the scale of the Universe. Let us not be deceived that evolution means the denial of entropy. It does not. The increase in life's complexity over the eons required energy, inevitably incurring an increase in entropy. That was the price paid for the complexity and consciousness we have today over trilobites. We cannot expect something for nothing. As for the complexity built up, life on Earth is only in a temporary space-time zone, fed by the benevolent energy flow from our Sun. Eventually entropy will overcome this benevolence when our Sun expands billions of years in the future and our Earth will rejoin the normal river of time in the Universe, destroying all life on it. Time is the destroyer of worlds (Bhagavad-Gita 11:32).

Intelligent life, however, has hope, for at that distant future our species' descendants will have learned to escape the inevitable fate of our Earth by moving elsewhere, to another stellar system where they can continue. Indeed, the same will happen long before then, since the Mission of Man is to seed the galaxy[6]. If intelligence exists elsewhere in the Universe we can imagine the same happening. Intelligence is distinguishable by being able to avoid entropic regression, as when we avoid accident and sickness, or create. Although as yet rare, life will eventually come to dominate the Universe, and we can speculate that when entropy is maximum so will be intelligence.

Emergence is another feature of complex systems that becomes apparent at higher scales, where a system displays wider and more complex properties than were evident, or even suspected possible, on the scale of its individual agents. An individual ant or bee gives no clue to its complex colony potential, nor when looked at under a microscope does a single neuron suggest anything possible like a human mind

---

6 Someone calculated that by sequential colonizing from one star to the next, humanity could have our entire galaxy colonized in fifty million years, which is the blink of an eye in the lifetime of a galaxy.

when composed into a neural network. The cells of our bodies do indeed form a whole greater than the sum of their parts. Throughout the history of life we see cellular emergence, from chemical molecules to one-celled organisms, jellies, fish, amphibians, reptiles, mammals and humans, each stage in evolution displaying higher complexity. We can extrapolate the process far into the future, to the realization of a *Cosmic Imperative*[7] – the self-organization of *Ultimate Life*. Human beings can choose to be conscious participants in that Cosmic Imperative, or they can blindly ignore it and like animals live their lives blissfully unaware of any higher aim than their individual existence, or they can choose to retard and even reverse the emergence of higher life. The choice they make defines their morality.

Thus is explained the divide between yin and yang, the destructive and creative forces in the Universe. Although entropy must ultimately consume Creation, our moral duty is to struggle against it, because by doing so we can salvage a small part of Creation whereby Ultimate Life can arise. We might think there is contradiction between entropic regression and the Cosmic Imperative, having stated that both are in opposition and inevitable, but there is none, since one is born from randomness with chance in its favor and the other from overwhelming numbers that submerge random chance. The room of a house with usage becomes messy, that is inevitable, which is not to say it will not be cleaned. With a fastidious housekeeper that cleaning is inevitable too, and although we might think there is nothing inevitable about a fastidious housekeeper, by the laws of probability in a limitless Universe where all is possible even that will inevitably arise.

---

7 In the language of Complexity Theory: a *strange attractor*.

III

What is beauty? Beauty relativists tell us that human beauty is culturally dependant, governed by our conditioning. Undoubtedly some truth resides in this view, but the question was explored scientifically by researchers who found that our perception has a more absolute foundation. Photographs of faces were given college students for beauty evaluation, where it was found that people considered good looking had the most facial symmetry. Left and right sides most resemble each other. In other words, the human mind interprets spatial order as beauty. The criterion of symmetry cannot be applied for the profile, but a good-looking profile, most seem to agree, is the straight profile with a 'firm' chin and no prognathism (muzzle mouth). It is the profile most evolved from the ape profile, and again the mind's perception of beauty is an appreciation of the Creative principle in the Cosmos.

In the same way, from our understanding of material nature we can glean an insight by analogy into human nature. What exactly *is* a 'good' person? Obviously he/she is one whose activities are helpful in fostering the well being of his/her family, friends, community and society, all being pursuits working against entropic regression in the human condition. The more celebrated in this category are popular leaders when social corruption and tyranny are defeated, inventors and discoverers who give a better material existence to mankind, thinkers who elevate our understanding, and moral philosophers who admonish our animal natures. In other words, what is felt by people to be 'good' behavior is that which promotes the Cosmic Imperative, so we are not surprised that qualities we consider 'good,' such as honesty, further society and human life. Since that behavior helps to promote higher order, manifested in an improved humanity, 'good' behavior is only realized through effort, that is, by the expenditure of energy.

An analysis of *morality* now becomes clear. The human being has inherited much of the instinct and passion of the animal, that was indispensable for survival of the animal but in people can be the cause of waste, destruction and neurosis. Evolution means the development of life away from the position where survival is a matter of chance with a high degree of dependency on the environment. It is the process whereby animals gain a measure of freedom from the arbitrariness of Nature, and modern people have gained or are gaining complete mastery of their environment. The question, then, can be raised whether the evolutionary process has at last ended, with the present day human its final product. Control over external Nature has simply signaled the end of animal evolution; what remains is *human* evolution, meaning control over *internal* nature. Moral behavior means nothing more than this inner control over the emotional, animal part of one's nature, requiring energy as in the effort needed for self control when one's anger has been provoked. Humanity cannot raise itself further on the evolutionary scale by devising ever more sophisticated gadgetry; that can only be done by the force of internal *will*, which signifies cerebral control over the passions that are dictatorial in the animal, and thereby gain a freedom unknown to the animal kingdom. Greed, lust and egoism are not rational drives; they belong strictly to the emotional, animal, sphere. The purely carnal person is one with little cerebral control over feelings and desires, similar to an animal. Being closer to the animal, the immoral person has a lower order of character than the virtuous.

Not to be understood is that morality means the elimination of emotion, that would robotize the sensitive human experience. To make an understanding of this point concise, we may take the example of hunger. Man's need for food is physical, and to deny that need with lengthy fasting is destructive of the body. Although destructive, fasting is not considered immoral, some sects even practicing it in their religious excesses. Obesity, on the other hand, is also destructive of the body, but in addition carries the suggestion of moral weakness. Why this difference if both are destructive? Whereas the ascetic practices cerebral control over his/her body, the obese has surrendered to animal craving. But this is only to say that obesity is immoral, not that the ascetic is acting morally when practicing restraint beyond the limits of practical judgment. In the same sense, to deny or subvert the emotional side of life is also destructive. Just as modern people cause destruction to their external world when they exercise control without respect for Nature or environment, causing dire consequences for themselves, so do they with regard to internal nature. Discipline over the emotional self means *channeling* rather than denying the instincts inherited from our evolutionary past, and in this manner creative pursuits can receive immense impetus derived from emotional involvement. In the same way that we can bring greater beauty to external Nature with parks and gardens, by controlling our inner nature we can also beautify, and express those cultivated feelings creatively. Thus there is a great similarity between the broadest interpretation of morality and *culture striving*. Both are expressions of inner mastery unknown to the animal world.

Evil behavior, conversely, denotes behavior that ultimately is motivated by selfishness with no social benefit, that is parasitical and therefore associated with little or no personal achievement. It connotes no effort in creative pursuit; a thief produces nothing except misery for those whose labor has gone into provision. Evil people by definition cause harm and destruction, and since without creative effort the fate of the world is entropic regression, they are agents of decay acting in time. This understanding of evil is not a discovery of *Cosmos Theology*, being intuitively felt since the dawn of history. The Egyptian god of evil, *Set*, was also the god of *chaos*. The meaning is not that entropic regression is the *cause* of evil, but rather that evil is our interpretation of human activity conducive to disorder in the world. The mind is constructed to respond to such behavior with feelings, not analysis. Good and evil are concepts of the mind, as is beauty. Just as we interpret a high degree of spatial order as beauty, we interpret agents of entropic regression, those who give it *intent*, as 'evil,' and agents of order, those who build society and aid human life, and hence are agents of the Cosmic Imperative, as 'good'.

The connection between 'evil' and entropy can most readily be seen in the case of cancer. Certainly cancer is considered 'evil,' causing suffering and death as well as the social cost of billions of dollars spent on its cure when people are afflicted with this dreaded malady. Environmental agents and life-style are contributors, but the one major cause is aging. Our bodies' cells must replicate, and throughout our lives random mistakes occur in our personal DNA that cause our cells to mutate. The longer we live the more mutations our bodies carry. Here is entropic regression in action. Some mutations cause cells to continue growing, and we develop cancer. Our bodies' entropy simply means *evil* by another name.

We therefore see the lack of any need for personalized good and evil that people believe derive from a spirit world. Good behavior is simply behavior that contravenes entropic regression in human affairs, that acts in harmony with universal Creation, is order constructing and must by necessity require energy in the form of effort and struggle. Evil is nothing more than the active compliance with the decay of time in human affairs. There is nothing spiritual or metaphysical in this understanding, nor any need to invoke 'higher' powers from an unseen world; the understanding is an act of simple, everyday intelligence, not of profound and unfathomable faith. Of course, we could still assume mysterious powers behind good and evil, but once explained rationally such views become superfluous.

Apart from spiritual notions, a subjective understanding of ethics derives from whether people *know* their behavior is destructive or degrading of humanity. If they have that knowledge all will agree that the behavior is unethical, but the question of subjectivity arises because this knowledge is not always present. In a hedonistic culture a dissipative lifestyle may be considered "good" if everyone is having a "good time," and the celebrated may be the popular entertainers who glorify that life-style. Human approval is very plastic, which we can see in many cases, such as when considering that tolerance towards drugs can be reversed in different societies, where their use can have total social acceptance in one culture but cause imprisonment in another. Foods eaten in some countries are considered disgusting in others. Some primitive cultures have thought little of cannibalism. Most societies in the world have been patriarchal, but on the Caribbean isle, Isla de Mujeres, the rule of women is felt entirely natural. There are polygamous as well as monogamous societies, where usually it is men who have several wives, but societies also exist where polyandry is practiced by women who have several husbands. Some nations practice arranged marriages, a practice thought in the West to be a severe restriction on personal choice. Sex has been equated with immorality in monotheistic cultures, which is quite different from the more relaxed attitude toward sex among nonChristian and nonMoslem peoples. Kama Sutra was an East Indian religious doctrine of extensive sex, which left such graphic carvings that Mahatma Gandhi wanted its temples destroyed. Our Western condemnation of homosexuality would have been out of place in ancient Greece. In ancient Chaldea the temple was a place of prostitution and business. There are twenty nations in Africa where parents insist on clitorectomy of their young daughters. In all these examples the practices have been thought justifiable, moral and even necessary. Vikings and Mongols glorified war and violence. Pre-Columbian Mexicans practiced human sacrifice by the thousands. Suicide has long been honorable in Japan, as it was in the ancient world, but felt tragic in Western countries. Gladiatorial combats were common in Roman times, but would not be tolerated today as a civilized form of entertainment. That two societies could have such different moral views on the fate of individuals shows that even sentiments about life and death are not embedded in our human make up. We could think of the uproar in the modern world if crucifixion were employed as a means of capital punishment, yet in the ancient world it was, and thousands died in that gruesome manner. Regardless of the high caliber of philosophical thought in the Greco-Roman world, not one philosopher of that time condemned slavery. They could not because ancient society was based on it; the Roman Empire was a slave empire, and again we see the inconsistency of moral standards in the public conscience, which can vary from acceptance in one society to outrage in another. In an era before automatic engines were invented, economic pressures to maintain slavery must have been considerable, but eventually proved no match against the moral demands of the early Church. Even so, the practice took ages to die out, serfdom, even under the Church, was little different, and the pressures were always present, evidenced by the American South. Confederate armies fought as hard to preserve the Southern "way of life" as Union armies fought to destroy it. Many examples can be given of people who believe their behavior is acceptable, or at least not evil, and therefore good and evil can be though relative, based on different circumstances.

Is the atheist's judgment of subjective right and wrong correct after all? It certainly can be given weight from a humanistic perspective. The humanist tradition runs deep within the atheist movement, so without belief in an all-powerful Lawgiver atheists have no trouble accepting a subjective version of good and evil. It is when we attempt to find the place of human behavior in Nature that we gain superior insight. After all, there is more to moral acceptance than emotional perception. In the long evolution of human life the beliefs of people must have tapped into the realities of the world, or they would never have survived. All of the above examples can be judged according to their benefit or injury to humanity, that is, on whether they are conducive to human advancement or not, so we are still left with an absolute standard – the Cosmic Imperative. In the case of slavery, for instance, if before the invention of automatic machines society could have advanced equally well without it, then slavery was absolutely immoral. Could we say the same if society could not have advanced equally well without it? Slavery released talented people from toil, to perform the art, science and philosophy for which the Classical World is noted. Would it have been 'good' to deprive humanity of that progress, even in part? That would not have been in accord with the Cosmic Imperative, so we do not see the philosophers of the Classical World condemning the slavery of their time. Black slavery of the American South, however, occurred at a time when automatic machines were taking over human labor, and made slavery a less efficient means of production. Human advancement would therefore have been retarded by the continuance of slavery, and hence the moral repugnance against it, but we can be assured that without automatic machines slavery would still be prevalent in the world today, and moral arguments would be given from pulpits to justify it, as they were in the old South.

We can empathize with the plight of human beings, but surely our understanding must extend beyond, to a deeper understanding of the world we live in. This is where religion enters, which if mistaken about Nature, as mythical and mystical teachings are likely to be, can be evil even if in the guise of holiness. Vows of poverty, for example, from the point-of-view of humanity and life's imperative, are sacrifices that lead nowhere. Individuals can believe they are doing 'good,' yet seen holistically their practice lessens the strength and viability of humanity, especially if proclaimed ideologically *en masse* with potential to beget nations of beggars. From the viewpoint of the Cosmic Imperative people can be sadly mistaken. It is by their effect *on the scale of humanity,* on whether they promote or retard human advancement irrespective of human tragedy, that notions of good and evil must be judged, and that measure is absolute, not relative.

Although societies have different moral perceptions, if

mistaken and moral philosophers do not address those mistakes, the society will learn by experience. In Western society we consider monogamy to be the moral standard for marriage, which the moral relativist would say is dependant on our cultural bias because Arab societies practice polygamy with no moral qualms whatever. One study, however, found that polygamy causes a more violent society due to male competition for brides[8]. If a wealthy man can have four wives at the same time, that leaves three men without any wife. The result is that polygamy is slowly dying throughout the world. Evidently Nature decides the morality of a custom, not people, and we have to know what the rules are. If we do not we find out the hard way.

A querulous atheist will complain that placing the evolution of humanity as the centerpiece of morality does not answer why this should be judged 'good,' as humanity could be judged evil from the viewpoint of another species, so relative morality still applies. If microbial life is found on Mars, this reasoning goes, would humans have the right to replace that life by colonizing the planet? If so, would a superior alien species have the right to colonize Earth and replace humans? Here we could again have the argument that what is right or wrong depends on one's point-of-view. From the Cosmic Imperative, however, we need to first realize that any Martian life found is going nowhere evolutionarily. Conditions on Mars do not allow for further evolution than microbial. Human life on Mars would be an advancement, and may even be a requirement for long term survival of our species from its dispersal, since we know from the past history of our planet that near extinction of life on Earth is possible. Human colonization of an Earth-like exoplanet in another solar system, conversely, would be an

8 University of British Columbia News, January 23, 2012

outrage if that planet were found to be in the early stages of life as was Earth two billion years ago. To destroy or impede that life's development would be contrary to the Cosmic Imperative, and in this light so would be any alien colonization of Earth.

This is not to say that humanity cannot be evil. Indeed, we see during our present time humanity responsible for the extinction of many species in our world, estimated to be between 0.01% and 0.1% of all species per year, for which geologists have named this Age of Man the "Anthropocene." Forests are cut down, habitats are lost, ecosystems are ruined, entire fish stocks are depleted with pollution now causing vast dead zones in the world's oceans, and climate change caused by human economic activity threatens to turn Earth's atmosphere into another Venusian one. The end of it all can only mean that humanity itself will suffer. Surely a species like this from the Cosmic perspective cannot be considered 'good'. If we do not learn to act more wisely with our home planet we can be assured that catastrophe is in the making, but we should not think that the end of humanity would invalidate the Cosmic Imperative. It would only be a failure in our small corner of the galaxy. In the far reaches of space and time the Cosmic Imperative would still operate among more morally responsible species.

For an appreciation of *Cosmos Theology* we must judge morality from a genuine *Cosmic* perspective, not with a limited human and therefore subjective vision. The sacrifice of other species can be justified when in conflict with human advancement, but not when other options are available since most species except parasites are a denial of entropy, and this includes extraterrestrial life, if ever found. To destroy life on an exoplanet would clearly be against the progress of life in the Universe since humanity would gain no particular benefit, there being many future opportunities for humanity on the scale of the galaxy. *Within* humanity the same rule could not historically be applied, because it is by competition *within* species that evolution has advanced. Cultures that lose will not agree on how to achieve ends that are 'good'. Understandably they will take subjective views. At its most primitive that subjectivity is at the individual level, but in tribes some of that individual subjectivity had to be sacrificed for a more co-operative collective. When tribes advanced into nations that tribal subjectivity had to be shed. A united humanity will have lost all subjectivity and finally absolute 'good' will be realized – that which promotes all humanity as an emerging social species participating in the Cosmic Imperative.

Actually, everyone has intuitive knowledge about the difference between good and evil, between morality and immorality, and that is because everyone knows the difference between animal and human thinking. We all have intuitive awareness of our 'inner ape' and how control over our animal selves is the basis for moral behavior, which is not to say we always use that gift. Circumstances and cultures can be different, but human versus animal behavior remains the criterion for judgment, and although primitive cultures can exalt their animal virtues, that is one reason why advanced cultures consider them primitive, so when animal needs become secured the acceptance of animal practices tends to disappear in cultures over extended periods. If not, such customs will cause their less competitive societies to be destroyed, eliminating those customs. Asking how humanity knows good and evil is like asking how humanity knows what is beneficial for itself. Sometimes, in fact most of the time, it does not. It learns from experience. The individuals and tribes that did not learn good from evil in the past were out-competed and probably exterminated. We are still learning, and that is why we have confusion, even wars, over good and evil.

Of course, a lot of considered moral practices do not involve personal instinct and emotion, being designed more to regulate society. There is nothing emotional about driving on the right side of a street rather than the left. But even here there is a connection in the grand scheme of life, because without rules we would have chaos and social regression. Acting like an ape means nothing more than entropic regression to a less evolved state. It is all connected by the same overriding principle. Humanity sees this, realizes that entropic regression, whether in behavior or rule braking, is not conducive to its well being, and has labeled it 'evil'.

At the individual level, the connection between entropic regression and unethical behavior is evident. If a pedestrian is run over by a car everyone will agree that the act was evil if done deliberately, but not if caused by the car's brakes failing, regardless of the result being the same: someone was hurt or killed. We would think the same if the accident was caused by drunkenness or carelessness or by any stupidity. If stupidity was *not* the cause and the accident was deliberate, how would we consider the driver? Would we not think of him/her as having committed evil? The only difference is the intent. Or we could take a more subtle example: a chair is an ordered arrangement that like all ordered arrangements subject to random forces in time will deteriorate. Given a hundred, two hundred or a thousand years the chair will become dust. When we are children we are taught (or should be taught) to have respect for someone's property, so if a child deliberately breaks a chair he/she is scolded. If a child attempts to repair a broken chair he/she is commended. Thus in actuality arises our understanding of proper and improper behavior. Clearly breaking the chair is in flow with time and for that reason is easy, even tempting for a mischievous child. Repairing the chair is an 'upstream' action against order regression and for that reason requires effort. To understand the relationship of evil to the decay of time it is first easier to remind ourselves that error is an agent of regression. Obviously mistakes do not improve matters. But *the effects of error and accident are the same as the effects of evil*. If the chair were broken by accident rather than by mischievousness the end result would be the same.

In examples like the chair someone's life is affected, the owner's, and from such experiences it is easy to derive that good and evil are subjective and depend on one's point-of-view. Perhaps the broken pieces of chair could be used for kindling to heat someone else's pot of water. Such arguments are always from restricted vision or from not considering the greater order to be achieved. If the subjective viewpoint is insisted upon, then let us look from the Cosmic viewpoint. We gain superior moral insight by having a more Cosmic perspective than emotional subjectivity. The demolition of a house may be against the wishes of its owner, and if its destruction were due to vandalism we can sympathize with the owner's judgment that the act was evil, a judgment entirely different if it were for public renewal. A thief may very well consider stealing to be 'good,' indeed, this author met a youth who was so convinced, but his subjective understanding is void of any understanding on the needs of society and what would happen if everyone were a thief.

The question of relative morality is answered by *emergence*. To destroy sickness-bearing microbes, insects and animals, although living beings, is not judged immoral because Man is closer to the ultimate attainment of Life than they, and in their threat to human life act as an impediment to the

Cosmic Imperative. Similarly in the case of war – should we condemn the empire building of nations throughout history, in view of their toll on human life in their construction? To answer we must judge whether the many empires that extended their dominance over large regions retarded humanity. When examined the case can be made that civilization today would be less advanced without having had them, with a few exceptions. Therefore they served a purpose in the grand scheme of Life, and this judgment would be made regardless of humanitarian considerations.

IV

Equipped with our understanding we can apply it in judgment of moral beliefs and practices, and modern schools of conduct. What, for example, can we make of the Biblical charge: ...*do not eat from the tree of knowing good and evil,...* (Genesis 2: 17)? Surely *Cosmos Theology* must proclaim: Let us eat from that tree, and eat heartily! We also read that God cursed Adam: *In the sweat of your brow you must make a living...* (Genesis 3: 19). *Cosmos Theology* shows that Man until the modern age had no recourse but to toil if he/she were to be a moral and responsible creature, since what is 'good,' being creative acts of Cosmic order and complexity, can only be achieved through effort and struggle. A moral code that denigrates work as a curse is hardly engendering of a prosperous mankind. To ally ourselves with the Cosmic Imperative we *must* adopt ethical behavior unavoidably associated with struggle that is necessary for the highly ordered state of life and its promotion. We *must* concern ourselves with our daily living, work to improve our material existence and not be frivolous with disposing wealth, act forcefully against corruption, do our best to ensure both personal and social survival and raise healthy generations for the future, if we are to act as moral beings. And with each of these duties is associated effort; that is inescapable with the construction of order.

As a moral doctrine, Christianity is lacking. Nowhere in the *Four Gospels* of Matthew, Mark, Luke and John does Christ teach the virtue of work, of caring for one's self or responsibility for one's family. On the contrary, he tells us: *Do* not lay up for yourselves treasures on earth...[9] (Matt. 6: 19); ...do not worry about your living - what you are to eat or drink, or about your body, what you are to wear. (Matt. 6: 25); Do not worry therefore, in view of tomorrow... (Matt. 6: 34). The analogy Christ draws is with ...the birds of the air, how they neither sow nor reap nor gather into barns, but your heavenly Father feeds them. (Matt. 6: 26). This passage demonstrates Christ's ignorance of Nature, for every animal is engaged in a struggle for survival, to feed itself, raise its young and ward off predators. In addition to not seeking wealth we should give away what we have: ...go and sell what you have and donate it to the needy,.. (Matt. 19: 21). Instead of being circumspect we should: Give to the one who begs from you and do not refuse the borrower. (Matt. 5: 42). We must also question Christ's pacifism: ...Do not resist injuries, but whoever strikes you on the right cheek turn to him the other as well. And if anyone wants to sue you for your tunic, let him have your robe as well. (Matt. 5: 39,40). Love your enemy, and pray for your persecutors, (Matt. 5: 44). His preaching against the family is most questionable: Whoever comes to Me without hating his father and mother and wife and children and brothers and sisters, yes, even his own life, cannot be My disciple. (Luke 14: 26). The sons of this world marry and are given in marriage, but those who are considered worthy of obtaining yonder world and the resurrection from the dead neither marry nor are given in marriage. (Luke 20: 34,35). Christ's rejection of sexual relations goes to the point of absurdity: ...and some have made themselves eunuchs for the sake of the kingdom of heaven. He that is able to accept it, let him accept it. (Matt. 19: 12). Christian doctrine has rationalized these verses, but knowing the celibate Essene background of Christianity and the fact that Christ himself was celibate, the

9 All quotations are from The Modern Language Bible, The New Berkeley Version.

most assured interpretation can be taken as they literally read. That Christ rejected all sexual relations is supported by Revelation 14: 4, where we are told that the 144,000 redeemed from the Earth are: ...*those who have not defiled themselves with women, for they are celibates.* The whole doctrine of the Four Gospels adds up to an unlivable imposition on the individual and society, so by the second century when the two Timothies were written, conventional morality regarding the family, child begetting and managing a household was reasserted (see Appendix C).

Mystical doctrines that preach renunciation and pacifism are divorced from the real world we experience. If one believes in an 'other world' that is higher than the present and is committed to attaining a purely spiritual existence, it is that spiritual world that has more meaning. Consequently, not to care for one's body, family and society, not to put full exertion into practical achievement, automatically follows. We therefore have the implication that the very underlying principle of spiritual belief is iniquitous. Fortunately for society renunciation and pacifism have been the preserves only of saints and eccentrics, not of the more responsible elements of a population, because from our understanding of entropic regression we can be certain that if the tenets of Christianity had been followed when the masses of faithful faced cutthroats and con-artists, the world would long ago have been overrun by evil.

Innate human morality derives from construction of the human brain. The frontal lobes of the brain constitute the part that modifies emotions originating in the brain's primitive limbic system. It is the part of the brain involved in planning, organizing, problem solving, expectations, determination of consequences, and the ability to suppress urges. It is the most recently evolved part of the brain found most developed in humans, the seat of guilt and our humanity, which all human beings possess. Lasting moral teachings are only those that conform to this 'inner light' of ours, and empathy.

As a result of our inner guidance we do not need religion to teach rightful behavior, shown by some of the most ethical people in the world being atheists. We can instinctively judge behavior that is in accordance either with the Cosmic Imperative or entropic regression, including when the effects of good or evil are subtle. For example, what about personal hygiene? Without it the assault on our noses is unpleasant but is that sufficient for labeling the lack of hygiene immoral? The Bible makes frequent mention of cleanliness, as in Ezekiel 36:33 – ... *On the day that I cleanse you from all your iniquities,* ... suggesting the morality of "cleansing," unfortunately without explaining why. We can now understand why, and are given a more rational moral outlook than from mystical proclamation: *Thus says the Lord God.* Filth accumulates in time and is inevitable with the play of disorder in our lives. With habitual cleanliness we act contrary to that inevitability, and like all activities against time's randomness it requires effort. As followers of this principle we are morally obliged to practice cleanliness. It is the same with all examples of personal morality, including laziness. Here is another case where immoral behavior is perceived but not specified in conventional religion. First, we realize that lack of desire to work does not always imply laziness. People who are old, tired or in ill health do not want to work because of physical inability. It is the person who makes no effort although able to work who is considered morally deficient, and again we see the implication of energy expenditure in questions of moral behavior. The lazy and especially the slovenly take so little charge of their affairs as not to act against random influences on their daily lives. It is this lack of *will* to act against the pervasiveness of Cosmic regression on the individual scale that sets them apart from moral society, and on their consequent, inevitable path to personal decline.

We can bring our understanding to bear on modern social issues, including environmentalism. Obviously nutritious food free from contaminants and a healthy environment have an importance for human life, so if an industrial project means the destruction of farmland, or of lands required for the survival of wildlife, we know it is regressive of the general welfare of our world even if done in the name of progress. Can we say the same of an industrial project where environmental degradation is possible but every effort is made to *avoid* it? Laying a pipeline is different from the previous example because in that case no doubt was incurred – the farmland would be destroyed – whereas in the second case the destruction would be accidental. That possibility is unavoidable with *any* human enterprise. To drive a car invites accident, to light a fire runs the risk of being burned, to leave our mothers' wombs is the most dangerous event of our lives. Although qualitative assessments are sensible to make, in general to thwart economic progress from the fear of accident is an insult to the human spirit and not what we would expect for the advancement of humanity.

An issue bearing on personal morality is sex. Why has sexual relationship required religious consecration in all societies the world over? Why has marriage been deemed moral? More pointedly, why has sex been condoned within the marriage bond yet condemned outside of it? If condemned in one instance and condoned in the other it cannot be the act itself that has religious concern. One obvious function sex has is procreation. The choice of a marriage partner is made with more discrimination than of someone for a 'one night stand' when qualities of mind and character need hardly be considered. If marriage were not a social institution and the renewal of generations were entirely open, this element of selection would be removed and population renewal would be more randomized. Marriage pairs people according to abilities, interests and socioeconomic status, the best marrying the best, and when children must be supported by the family with no support by the state, *selection* in marriage tends to proportionately increase the number of favorable children in a population. Apart from men not abandoning their responsibility in support of women, marriage works against entropic regression in eugenic caliber. Tribes in the past that practiced marriage therefore out competed tribes that did not, and due to natural selection among tribes marriage became ubiquitous among the most competitive, whose members became our ancestors. In marriage we see a direct connection between a moral custom, survival and the Cosmic Imperative.

A poignant moral decision facing modern society will bring our standpoint into further focus: the issue of abortion: is it moral, immoral or amoral? The policy of some church denominations is blanket condemnation, based on human life judged sacred. The humanist believes the issue revolves around human rights and freedoms, in particular the right of women to having control over their own bodies. The sacredness of human life and the rights and freedoms of people both seem to be reasonable grounds for ethical proclamations. But something is wrong, or our understanding of ethics is incomplete if both are correct. We would think that two paths to ethical understanding would not conflict. With our enlightenment we can seek a resolution:

It is evident that life manifests an ordering process and should generally be viewed sacred, with the exception of parasites that are themselves detrimental to life in obvious accord with entropic regression. When a fetus threatens the life of the mother, or is infirm in some manner that its support after birth would mean a constant and unrepaid sacrifice on the part of its parents or society, its growth is no longer a social investment but is purely parasitical and means a weaker social whole with its fulfillment. The support of a weak baby in a family of limited resources may mean that the family foregoes a strong baby. Poverty means a lessening of life, and families that are too large, nations that are unable to support their masses, behave neither rationally nor ethically when they increase their numbers still further. Thus, abortion and all measures of birth control can be ethically justified when numbers prey upon themselves, or when any form of life preys upon the strength of the whole. But in the same category can we place abortion for convenience, i.e., abortion or birth control simply because children would impinge upon the life-style of their not-to-be parents? Clearly in this case there is lack of recognition for the basic struggle that is unavoidable in all order creation, and it is in this renunciation to maintain the struggle of life where lies the unethical premise of induced sterility, of purposeful childless marriages and convenient celibacy. It is in this light that a pregnancy brought to an artificial termination is the result of a selfish decision. Clearly a woman has the right to control over her body, but it could be argued as well that a man's freedom is equally limited when he has a family to support, yet no one would argue that he stifle or abandon his children for this reason. The family reduces the freedom of both, which demonstrates how freedom and the whole issue of individual and democratic rights cannot be the criterion for judging ethical behavior. Just as the Universe gave us life we have a duty to return life to it. Deliberate sterility, the denial of worthy human life to the Universe, is hardly conducive to the Cosmic Imperative.

A major problem induced when birth control is widely available and practiced is a eugenic one, because it is then college-educated women who practice it, thereby limiting their numbers in a population more so than women who are less mindful of conception. When in addition the children of welfare families are supported by the state, meaning a transfer of resources through taxes from society's producers, a situation is set up for the proliferation of an intellectual under class at the cost of society's mainstays. The childlessness of the present Western world is particularly conducive to such a eugenic crash since Western countries generally seek to replace their missing numbers with immigrants from abroad, opening them to the possibility of a dysgenic trend. Italy is an example, whose own population has an average I.Q. of 102 but is being replaced by immigrants from countries where the population I.Q. average is in the mid 80s. Even in the matter of population intelligence we see the pervasive influence of entropic regression – the trend to decline over time when there is no force to prevent it.

The function of traditional religion has been to give people a place in the Cosmos and to direct behavior in accordance with laws conceived to be universal and natural. With the end of traditional belief this point of reference is lost; people then become their own point of reference, and ethical behavior depends on what promotes the rights and happiness of individuals. Like traditional religion, a rational religion need have no basis in humanism, and may reach conclusions contrary to the requirements of individual happiness. Competition in sport, politics and business places stress and strain on individuals, but we cannot condemn competition because of such undesirable effects; these are to be expected in the human struggle.

Normally, in our everyday lives, judgment on behavior depends on the effects of that behavior. If an act causes harm to more people than it helps, it is considered unethical. If the level of harm caused to a few is higher than the amount of good bestowed upon many, the act may still be considered unethical although a qualitative assessment becomes necessary. Religion is not exempt from this 'common sense' view of ethics, as in the Buddhist/Confucian/Christian Golden Rule: "Do unto others as you would have them do unto you." It would seem that 'common sense' is the perfect guide, except that we must wonder if 'common sense' is a universal guide for all cases. To find out, we'll analyze three issues perplexing modern society, each hinging on our treatment of people: the abolishment of capital punishment, homosexuality and multiethnicism, to see if their acceptance possesses internal, logical difficulties. If they do, the Golden Rule breaks down, and it will not be surprising if we find they are in accord with entropic regression. Instead of immediately analyzing each in the light of that law, however, we'll pull them together under one label and see if that general category is or is not a product of time.

Capital punishment is an issue certainly directed against the personal interests and happiness of criminals. A case can be made against it when there is the least doubt of guilt because the punishment is irreversible, but with increasing sophistication of forensic techniques such doubt is becoming less problematic. What of capital punishment in cases where there is absolute certainty of guilt? Should the known guilty have their lives respected at public expense? Opposition to capital punishment in such instances is based on the notion that human life is sacred, and since criminal life is also human life, criminal life is included sacred. Presumably human life is considered sacred because it is intelligent life, a position that does not explain why intelligent life should be sacred when that intelligence is used for evil purposes. If an individual's value system does not permit control over greed, egoism and passions of all description, might we not question whether the life of that individual is on an animal plane rather than a human one?

From a different perspective we might say that what is sacred is humanity. Criminal life is part of humanity, but a part is not the same as the whole. In varying degrees criminal life threatens humanity. But something sacred cannot threaten something else that is sacred, because that would mean it is evil, which is impossible. Therefore criminal life cannot be sacred. What the humanist fails to understand is that destroying evil is not evil, irrespective of that evil taking human form.

The issue of homosexuality is another where the mores of society can impinge upon the rights, freedom and happiness of individuals. Here we must distinguish between the homosexual as an individual and homosexuality as a condition. An individual who stutters, for instance, cannot be condemned, which is not to say we must look favorably on the condition of stuttering. Society cannot condemn aberrant behavior of any type when that behavior is non-threatening and is victimless. That behavior need not be approved but neither can it be punished, especially when the individuals concerned have no choice in being what they are. There are several diverse factors that go into making homosexuals, but what is coming more to light is the role played by heredity, since it is found that male homosexuality runs in families, inherited from the side of the mother. Placental changes caused by the number of previous brothers may also be a cause. If womb influenced, the homosexual as an individual is blameless, and to ostracize him or her for the sexuality given by Nature is morally dubious.

The effects of a manner of conduct may be unknown until observed on a large scale, and to make a judgment on homosexuality as a condition all we need to do is exaggerate its occurrence in society. The condition at the individual level can then be judged a matter of degree. Any community composed entirely of pure homosexuals would last only one generation. If all humanity were so composed the same fate would befall it. Pure homosexuality on a mass scale would therefore make humanity less viable as a species. Like all conditions that weaken humanity, its morality as a condition becomes less certain, and proclamations on its normality must be questioned.

Yet another issue that impinges upon the rights and happiness of individuals involves race. In the modern era racial-cultural nationalism no longer exists in Western countries, these being open to immigration irrespective of racial origins. The main justification for multiculturalism is its diversity, which must include racial diversity since this is what brings the diversity in culture. Races around the world have blended together in various proportions to produce more variety than had there been no such mixture, the analogy being a painting with its mixture of colors. The difference, of course, is that by throwing nations open to the world and having no barriers to race migration, the end of diversity must eventually result. When people live without national barriers, history shows they blend. Like a painting where colors are continuously mixed, producing a toned down graying effect, the end of nationhood will not give a world of variety but one of racial-cultural sameness: the end of diversity. Proponents of multiculturalism are therefore caught in a logical dilemma.

The many examples of racism around the world in diverse cultures seem to support the view of universal racial consciousness, contrary to the notion that racism is purely a white phenomenon resulting from colonialism. It is therefore the individuals who step out of the norm and seek sexual partners from races not their own who must be viewed as having been politicized, who at some time in their lives have learned preference for the foreign, rather than the racially inclined having learned preference for their own. Again this view would seem to be supported by the facts, since the known statistical fact is that people marry partners with characteristics close to their own, including looks. A study reported in the research journal, *Psychological Science,* February 2006, found that three-month-old babies prefer faces of people from their own race to those of other races, and previous studies found that infants tend to recognize faces from their own race better than those from other races. If intolerance is learned it seems to be learned very easily, suggesting that it is the multiculturalist who must overcome an innate tendency, a development that is not only possible but probable in caring people when feelings of racial guilt are taught. So, from a moral point of view we might ask: which is more moral if morality is the exercise of control over our animal selves: yielding to racial instinct or restraint of racial instinct? At first glance it may seem that the anti-racist has the moral high ground, and indeed he/she makes this claim, loud and clear. But again we must remember the fine line between control and suppression, how control can be exaggerated into suppression and how suppression can result in our destruction. The control of sexual passion is generally considered moral, for example, but to suppress sexual passion to the point of not breeding is foolish. Analogously, to desire the preservation of one's biological as well as cultural heritage seems a proper exercise of instinct, well in accord with the variation of Nature, whereas the denial of that desire, that leads to the passing of one's heritage, must also be seen foolish. We should never forget that the instincts given us by Nature are for our survival. The mistake of the multiculturalist is seen from it being the sense of oneness with one's partner and children that leads to genuine feelings of *love*, whereas the more carnal appetite is satisfied with the titillation of difference, making racially mixed relationships suspect of being on a more animal level.

Along this same line we might ask about the "new world order" espoused by modern politicians, and the whole issue of world government premised on the ideal of "multiethnic nations". There can be little doubt that with developments in transportation and communications, the evolution of economic blocs and the danger to the world posed by nuclear weapons, that the globe is approaching some form of supranational government, but does this government necessarily need the ideal of "multiethnic nations"? Could not world government be a development among ethnic nations as well as "multiethnic nations"? World government, should it ever arise, need not be an imposition on nationhood, but the type of world order we are marching toward under the United Nations with plutocratic sponsorship surely will be. The tragedy it poses is that it will be a realization of a declining civilization, not unlike the Roman Empire that similarly melted together the nations of the ancient world. The current push toward the same nationless form is viewed the most obvious and natural undertaking once the requirement of a supranational structure is recognized, but that it will also be a degenerate manifestation of a dying world we know from the fate of the Roman Empire.

The issues of abolishing capital punishment, of acceptance of homosexuality and multiethnicism show how some trends in the modern world possess internal difficulties when placed under examination, with little reference made to entropic regression, but there is a common thread through them all: they are *liberal* issues. The essential premise of each is human happiness with emphasis on the individual, on his/her rights and privileges, but as was shown, a rational ethic need have no basis in a purely humanistic consideration. We may deplore the sacrifice of life in war, which says nothing about the morality of allowing a nation to be overrun by tyranny. Individual welfare cannot be the highest good when the collective welfare must take precedence. From the philosophical principle of utilitarianism (the greatest good for the greatest number), to expect the individual to sacrifice in service of a greater and more enduring collective cannot be improper, irrespective of his/her rights and happiness. But the sanctity of the individual is the unstated premise of modern liberalism, an emphasis suggesting diminution of collective interest without which no society can survive. The actual meaning is loss of the forces propelling society and direct connection to social regression. In the modern world, liberalism has become the *philosophy of decadence*.

The trend to disorder, as a universal tendency when there is no contravening force, is evident in people's *psychological* disposition with the march of time just as much as in the physical aspects of Nature we have considered. As with fruit, with too much ripening it becomes rotten, liberalism has been a valuable historical movement in the Western world in the promotion of liberty, where it was realized that true freedom is only achieved with self discipline, but with emphasis on the individual, where his/her 'happiness' is paramount, it is not difficult to see how this same liberalism could degenerate into a libertine outlook with its eventual manifestation in hedonism. And just as in physical nature, whether considering the sophisticated idea of entropy or our lowly ink experiment, the end result of time's randomness is equalization, so is there an analogy with liberalism. Where social equality is attempted in the striving of the disadvantaged we see a creative performance, equality to the liberal is a state that he/she is willing to promote with reduction of the higher to meet the lower. The real achievements of liberals, whether in leveling government programs or those from a live-and-let-live attitude, result in an exhausted plane for all; their emphasis on individual rights and freedoms makes them catalysts of destruction actually prejudicial to the humanity they so favor. Apart from crusading humanitarians, liberals simply acquiesce to the easiest solutions. They support the natural course, and consider the natural trend "progressive" because it seems inevitable, lending their weight to the corrosive action of time.

V

How should we think of the Cosmic Imperative? The Universe is constantly changing. Stars continue to be born, and die. We live in a self-realizing Universe where Creation has never stopped. In the record we see evolution, from seas containing only single cell organisms that existed two billion years ago, to multi-cellular jellies, fish, amphibians, reptiles, mammals to Man. There is an evident progression in time from the simple to the complex, from lower forms of life and consciousness to the higher. Creation is not static; it is fluid and dynamic like a living being. The Universe is on-going and self-created – a process more than a thing. Therefore we should not think of the Universe as a creation, but itself as the *Creator*. The tangible Universe includes the stars of the firmament, the interstellar gas from which they are born, planets that give rise to life, all of Earth's creatures, Man, etc., all are the material manifestations of the Universe as Creator. As the Universe carried along this Path of Creation each of its parts has served the Universal fulfillment, and the value of each has been its potential in that service.

We can extrapolate the progression far into the future. Before Man the Universe was blind: cosmic gas clouds could not foresee the suns that they were to become. Life evolves but its various forms are oblivious to how, by simply partic-ipating in the struggle for survival, they play a role in the advancement of life and the Cosmic Imperative. Man has served Creation in this same blind way through instinct, but now potentially in an enlightened and conscious way. If over past eons we see a progression toward consciousness, a reasonable conclusion is that the same progression will continue over future eons. The end result of this progression must be *Ultimate Consciousness*. The impulse in Nature toward that inevitable Destiny is the Cosmic Imperative, but let no one understand this argument to be teleological. If A, B and C occurred in the past, a reasonable assertion is that by the same process we can expect D in the future. Since Man is the present vanguard of that progress, over future eons life through Man will continue to evolve to ever-higher consciousness. From the animal realm has come Man, from Man will come Higher Man and from Higher Man will evolve Highest Life. *To participate in that progression of life is the interpretation humanity gives to the virtuous life.*

Just as the transition of life from ancient seas to land and from a world of reptiles to mammals were phase transitions in the long saga of life, so is the domination of the planet by Man another phase transition. With Man consciousness took a ratchet up, and with that consciousness has come the question of *meaning*. People seek meaning in their lives, and without it we are likely to see lives devoted to self-indulgence, to amusements, games and parties, drugs and stupefying intoxicants, and we must wonder if the motive for such abandonment is to divert their thoughts from that meaninglessness. Others attempt to give life meaning by garnering wealth, fame or power, or by becoming skilled in a craft, but unless these purposes serve in some way the Cosmic Purpose the lives of those who pursue them are meaningless and may as well never have been. It is the people of divine consciousness whose lives take on true meaning. The future evolution of life will unfold by Man *consciously* serving the Cosmic Imperative.

We could ask what form that evolution will take. Evolution does not pertain only to individual members of a species but also to groups with sophisticated functional integration. An example is a bee colony. Nectar patches are visited by single bees, and each bee returns to the hive with information on its patch found. It then does a dance to inform the hive about the direction and distance of the nectar patch. Colonies where individuals co-operated the best out competed colonies whose individuals had less communicative skill and co-operative behavior. That genetic endowment passed to each worker by the queen was selected over millions of years. Because that selection operated on the workers, in effect it was group selection.

Human beings also form groups. Nations, companies, clubs, etc. are examples of the human proclivity for joint action motivated by mutual interest. The strongest human groupings are those formed around moral systems. Religions sanctify ethical and moral codes that suppress narrow self-interest while promoting those that favor survival of the group. Religions provide rituals, dress and customs that solidify group cohesion. Religions give a transcendent meaning to life so their members feel part of a wider whole than just the immediate. By practitioners integrating their individualism into a collective, religions confer a survival advantage to their members. The in-group, collective constitution of religious denominations is an integral quality of those groups. Christians are mentioned as belonging to the "body of Christ" (I Corinth 12), Zen Buddhist monasteries have been constructed to resemble a human body, and both Mormon and Hutterite religions have referenced themselves to a beehive. In this latter property we see *emergence* – the complete integration of individual agents into higher complexity. It is such bonding, expressed in religious principles of charity, kindness and returning good for evil within an emergent social group that has evolutionary value. Through that evolution will be realized the Cosmic Imperative, not just as a religious idealization but as an actual living entity. By likening religious communities to living organisms, the Cosmic Imperative, although an evolutionary concept, is naturally adopted into a religious outlook.

That the evolution of future intelligence need not be thought of in strictly individual terms was confirmed by a study which measured the collective intelligence of groups and showed that such intelligence extends beyond the cognitive abilities of the groups' individual members[10]. The study involved 699 people placed in groups of two to five, given tasks on visual puzzles, negotiations, brainstorming, games and complex rule-based design assignments, and found that groups whose members had a higher level of social sensitivity were more collectively intelligent, irrespective of individual intelligence. Having a group of smart people does not necessarily make the group smart. Rather it is how well people perceive other's thoughts and feelings that produces better results. Significantly, the number of women in a group was an indicator of success. The groups where one person dominated scored low. Just as the collective intelligence of a beehive extends far beyond the intelligence of any one bee, human groups display the same collective superiority over atomized individuals, and therefore it would seem that this is the human form of intelligence most on the Cosmic Path. Although we can think of future human evolution resulting in Higher Man, we can also think of Higher Man in millions of years participating in a collectivity that as a single entity will constitute Highest Life.

---

10 Anita Williams Woolley, et al. (2010) "Evidence for a Collective Intelligence Factor in the performance of Human Groups." Science 330, 686.

By no means, however, should the development of a fully integrated religious body necessarily be thought the same as the development of a "hive" mentality, except if its members are under a controlling inducement, as could easily happen in the case of emotionally driven mystical religions. The very essence of enlightenment, as must be acknowledged, is an understanding of good and evil derived from Nature, that is, upon the exercise of personal intelligence and debate of its ideas rather than passive acceptance. Such a body lives up to the expectation of human ennoblement by encouraging, not suppressing, individual thought. Collectivism is then a product of individual edification when everyone is "on the same page," the result of truth found through rational learning, even science, perhaps mathematics, and therefore a most apparent philosophy on the Path of the Cosmic Imperative.

The usual reasons given for religion include it being a palliative against our natural fear of death, providing a reason for existence, giving a reason for doing good, etc., none of which answers why it should exist in Nature. How did religion begin? Nothing exists in Nature without having an efficient function honed by natural selection, and religion is extremely wasteful: martyrs leave few if any offspring, priests and clergy are of little economic benefit, the construction of temples consumes enormous resources yet no one lives in them. What possible biological advantage could religion bestow since its world wide prevalence seems to indicate a genetic disposition towards it, being found in every culture, climate and environmental circumstance?

The answer is given in the collectivity provided by religion: humans are a social species and *common* belief gives cohesion between people. Closely associated with religion are symbols, rituals and ceremonies that have the psychological function of cementing people together, especially do group practices where everyone participates such as in singing and praying. Undoubtedly belief can be a very personal matter in times of emotional difficulty, but if solace were the only reason for religion there would be no need for temples, churches and mosques. These are *meeting* places for *group* worship, and if they did not exist probably the religions would not either. So from the perspective of natural selection we must ask if common human bonding from religion has survival value. Of course, such bonding applies only to a *single* religion, not to a diversity of religions that historically has brought division to the extent of causing war and mass slaughter. Such division is caused more by the *breakdown* of religion, such as during the Protestant Reformation against Catholicism, and not by a *single, common* belief held by a population, treated here.

Following the thinking of biologist D. S. Wilson in *Darwin's Cathedral*, religious bonding does have survival value. Africa was the cradle of humanity, and Africa, with its droughts in the past was a difficult place to survive. In contrast to the billions of people in the world today, DNA examination has revealed that total human numbers at one time were down to only a few thousand individuals before dispersal of our ancestors throughout the world. Humans were a threatened species.[11] Under those conditions competition for resources was fierce, with our progenitors organized into hunter-gatherer bands of a dozen people or so each. Group cohesion was essential, so that any member who acted on his/her own to the detriment of the group could not be tolerated and was either immediately killed or expelled from a band, which meant the same fate. Those genes

11 We often hear the term human *race*. The term is a misnomer, used to politicize. Humanity is a species, composed of several races.

tended to be eliminated. Evidently that selection was successful to the point where today in modern Man it is not uncommon for injured players on a sports team to continue playing and risk permanent injury so as "not to let the team down". Astronauts have reported that their biggest fear is not death but of making a mistake that might jeopardize their mission.

Group natural selection has been disputed because the survival advantage of group cohesion with its altruistic requirement cannot have the survival advantage of our instinct for self-preservation, due to individual selection being on a shorter time scale than group selection. There is a distinct advantage in allowing others to do the sacrificing, a criticism that does not consider the social cost among humans of such selfish behavior. In competitive tribes and nations the *coward* is the most despised of men, who would be most noticeable in small bands, and if he happens to escape his commander's wrath his capital is still lessened as a mate. In small bands shirkers in general would be more noticeable, where they would gain sullied reputations reducing their mate potential. In small religious societies there must be something odd about the 'loner' who does not participate in religious practices. Pressure in the past would have been on self-centered individualism aiming at its elimination, while the altruistic and more socially conscious became more popular, even heroes. When group cohesion was an essential element in survival, the common practice of rituals and ceremonies in commemoration of tribal spirits, that served to unify early members of our species, gave their groups a competitive advantage. In this way an inclination for religion was a factor in our species' evolution.

Since religion gives psychological collectivism there should be no difficulty in recognizing its importance throughout history, even in the formation of collective enterprises we call civilizations. One historian, Oswald Spengler, wrote of civilizations (that he termed *high cultures*) as *organic* entities because they all have followed a similar, predictable pattern in their development. The most noticeable parallel is between the Classical World of Greece and Rome that developed around the Mediterranean, and the Western World of Europe and America that developed around the Atlantic, but the pattern is evident in the Mexican World of Maya and Aztec and all the civilizations of history (see Appendix B).

Social ideology is crucial in the life of civilization – all the great historical cultures began in religious periods when pyramids, ziggurats, temples and cathedrals were constructed, that employed much manpower indicating popular involvement. Those most monumental expressions of past civilizations were religious, and that cannot be coincidental. Then, all civilizations have shown a recurring psychological disposition, the same moving *Zeitgeist* as they matured, indicating that their development and aging cannot be due entirely to external influences. They are born, follow a similar life pattern, decay and die regardless of external circumstances. Certainly civilizations can be erased by environmental changes, from drought, for example, but if left to fulfill their historical course they seemingly follow a *biological* life cycle, determined purely by their internal destinies as intimated by Spengler. As with religious groups, we see *emergence* – the total integration of components into a higher order of complexity. Since religions have this function, we must wonder if civilizations are essentially religious constructions.

At the beginning of any civilization, in the words of historian, Carrol Quigley, people cannot be reorganized into a functioning society after the ruin of a previous one unless . . .

... they obtain a new nonmaterial culture and thus a new ideology and morale which serve as a cohesive for the scattered elements of past culture they have at hand. Such a new ideology may be imported or may be indigenous, but in either case it becomes sufficiently integrated with the necessary elements of material culture to form a functioning whole and thus a new society. It is by some such process as this that all new societies, and thus all new civilizations, have been born.[12]

We do not need to delve into deep history to discern the power of ideology for collective achievement. The Soviet Union was a case in point, where over 250 million people were propelled from a backward, agrarian society to the chief military threat of the West in a few decades. Yet Peter the Great, one of the ablest and most dedicated of rulers, failed to westernize Russia. The reason he failed was his inability to inspire the Russian masses with faith in his reforms; instead he actually antagonized the clergy and peasants with those forced innovations. Here we have insight into meaningful social change: *mass enthusiasm is essential.* This the Bolsheviks inspired by offering the hope of a "workers' paradise," backed by an invincible law of history. Once the fallacy of that hope was realized the Soviet Union fell apart, which was not necessary only from failed economics. The Soviet Union was above all an *ideological* construction. Much the same was evident with National Socialist Germany, that lasted only thirteen years, a time span within which that party, using a racial-nationalist ideology, took a defeated, depression racked nation and came within a hair's breadth of conquering Eurasia, then held off the world dur-

12 Carrol Quigley, *Tragedy and Hope*, page 14, The Macmillan Company, 1966

ing years of total war. Without possessing a collective faith society is atomized into its component individuals, who are without common motivation for mass enterprise and without extraordinary drive beyond personal want.

It is the same with spiritual belief as we find in the earliest agricultural phase of any "high culture," which will produce different results on society than a political ideology that produces results most identified with progress, but the earliest phase of any civilization is not marked by material advancement. The best known today of such epochs is the Middle Ages, when Gothic cathedrals were constructed and care was placed in religious art that resulted in the masterpieces of the Renaissance. The same is evident with all "high cultures": their beginnings are not notable by standards of common wealth and business enterprises, these are more characteristic of an aging civilization; rather the most profound cultural expressions of a young civilization bear a religious stamp.

A most evident example of the role of religion in the rise and flourishing of civilization was in the first cities of history, the Sumerian. The cities of ancient Sumeria were each totally dedicated to a god, as the city and its territory were considered the estate of that god and its inhabitants were looked upon as religious servants. The ranking of city importance did not depend on size of population, or on amount of commerce, but on the importance of the god it enshrined. Eridu was a holy city because it was the shrine of the god Enki, whom it was believed created mankind and the arts. The Lugal, or high priest of each city, issued orders for the maintenance of canals, fields, walls, workshops, etc., not in service of the city's people but of its god.

In Classical Greece also, every city-state had its own cult and favored deity: Athena of Athens or Diana of Ephesus.

Symbols of the gods were in every household, the dwelling of the king having a shrine. Every autumn the Athenians celebrated the Greater Mysteries, and after those celebrations, which lasted days, none less than the Senate met in extraordinary session to examine whether anyone was guilty of profaning those celebrations. Anyone guilty came under the threat of death. In 399 BC Socrates was condemned to death by the Athenians for his impious teachings regarding old beliefs. The Olympic Games originated more as contests to impress the gods than as athletic competitions. Pilgrims filled the sacred road leading to the hall of the Mysteries at Eleusis, some performing self mutilation, and as in every early society the great public buildings of Greece were temples, not government buildings or structures of business.

Even capitalism has not been untinged by religion in a dynamic way. Max Weber, in *The Protestant Ethic and the Spirit of Capitalism,* noted that all societies have had capitalism, but not all, if any before the West, have known it practiced as a calling, with an ethos beyond mere acquisition. Weber observed the people involved with the building of nineteenth century capitalism and found a total preoccupation with the making of money, more than necessary for the satisfaction of need or the quest of enjoyment. Wealth was an end in itself, motivated not by the fruits of possession, which were hardly considered, but by a belief that wealth was the ultimate purpose of life, to be pursued for its own intrinsic virtue. National qualities could not account for this conviction because his study of different motivations was among people of the same nation, Germany; rather he found that a difference in economic achievement divided between Protestants and Catholics. Even the type of education each received reflected different predispositions, Protestants preparing for middle class business life, Catholics preferring the humanities and crafts. Weber traced the economic orientation of Protestants to Calvinistic predestination, which taught that although an individual could not determine his/her salvation, one's worth could be known through works. The result was an induced work ethic that produced phenomenal capital expansion in Protestant lands, even after Calvin's original doctrine was forgotten.

There has been no paucity of theories on the rise and fall of civilization, these usually from an environmental or circumstantial perspective, reflecting the liberal disposition of present academia. There has been the *leisure* theory, which postulates that people will erect monuments, develop writing and evolve government only when some are relieved from constant toil. In contradiction there is the *hardship* theory, presented by historian Arnold Toynbee who suggested that civilization is a response to unpromising environments such as swamps, desert or broken terrain. The *climate* theory presents the notion that warm countries must be less advanced because of the lassitude a warm climate induces, apparently in ignorance of the historical fact that civilization began in warm countries, Iraq, Egypt and India. A popular paradigm today is that civilizations collapse because of environmental degradation, especially of soil infertility, yet Egyptian Civilization ended regardless of the Nile banks being renewed with annual floods. One of the more ludicrous of these 'resource depletion' hypotheses would have us believe that the Roman Empire fell because it ran out of slaves. Standing apart from environmental theories is the eugenic theory, which assumes that a racial population must have a minimum I.Q. to invent new ways of overcoming challenges. *All* these theories are premised on human *ability*. Of course the ability to build a civilization must exist, whether derived externally from the environment or internally from its human potential. Regardless of ability in all these theories there is one missing ingredient: *motivation*. Regardless of people's ability to build a city they must also *want* to build it, which is not obvious from our human desire for improved living. The most ideal society for human existence is that of the hunter-gatherer, where life is filled with family and socializing and requires little more than fourteen hours of work per week.

Environmental and eugenic factors obviously have an influence on the growth and sustainability of civilizations, but by also considering religion's importance to a growing culture we see that it cannot be ignored as a major contributor. Religion as a mass ideology has consequences in that it: 1) gives inner motivation for both individual and mass enterprise beyond immediate personal concerns, 2) directs people's attention toward specific goals, preparing them for unified action, 3) gives a 'world view' to the whole society. Commitment to a *Cause* separates a person from egoistic wants as an individual and places that person in the service of something above the self. People imbued with an ideology are self-sacrificing and look upon personal gratification as ignoble, upon materialistic preoccupation as a foolish concern. Any selfish or egotistical motivation cannot be identified with the Cause and is therefore secondary, or even a work of the devil. All striving is for the "glory of God," and any windfall, victory or promotion is by "Divine Will". By identifying with a collective body devoted to a holy Cause individuals share in the aspirations of that body and find a common peoplehood, promoting pride, hope, confidence and worth. Where there is an ideal concept, the ego is diminished; where there is a life purpose, there is aesthetic motivation; where there is a sense of belonging, there is energy for mass achievement.

At a deeper level of Nature than personal commitment and motivation, the connection between religion and civilization is given by *Complexity Theory*. Its startling revelation is that creation in Nature is realized by a delicate balance between the forces of stability and instability, at the interface between order and chaos, and these laws of pattern formation are universal, the mathematics is the same everywhere. We can expect civilization to be of the same genesis, meaning we should look for the same interplay of stability and instability within its structure, and we indeed find it in the tension between the individual with his/her freedoms, as the source of chaos, and of social ideology as the source of order. The progress of civilization comes from the balance between these two interests, from the individual who is ultimately the originator of discovery and invention, and from ideology that gives social motivation and structure. A nation of strong individuals will require a strong ideology, who because of their individualism will produce a dynamic society, but also because of their individualism without a strong ideology will be the more decadent and destructive of the civilization they construct. Social progress is realized in neither a state of barbarism nor in rigid ideological regimes. It is in the balance between freedom and submission, in deference, that "high cultures" unfold. We can postulate the permutations:

strong individualism + strong ideology ⇨ dynamic progress
weak individualism + strong ideology ⇨ stagnation
strong individualism + weak ideology ⇨ decadence
weak individualism + weak ideology ⇨ animal existence

An example of the first would be the Western world until the mid 20th century; of the second would be the ideological regimes of Islamic and Communist countries; of the third would be the present-day West; and of the fourth would be primitive areas of the third world where religion exists only as superstition, not collective dedication.

It is the psychological, value giving and motivational properties of a holy Cause, more than its moral teachings, that provide the underlying benefit of religion to a dynamic society. The religions of early "high cultures" in Asia, Carthage and Central America were absolutely immoral if we take the carnage of human sacrifice as an immorality. The Mayan religion was composed of the grossest superstition, with no ethical doctrine whatever. The licentiousness of ancient Babylonian religious tradition was scorned by the Hebrews, as it was by the Greek historian, Herodotus, yet Babylon was a dynamic focus of civilization. The Western world grew out of Christianity, which has moral teachings, but the humble serfs of the Middle Ages knew precious little of those teachings. The prime factor of religion is its *motivational idealism*, when people become secondary with their lives and possessions in the service of something above themselves. Thus we see massive efforts made in the expression of that idea, in stone, absorbing much manpower in spite of the meager homes and possessions of the people. Although the Egyptians were well advanced in stone masonry by 2900 BC, and construction of a Pharaoh's tomb required organization and trained leaders, the largest city of the time, Memphis, was built of sun baked brick and wood. To a materialist this is madness. No such idealism is evident in barbaric religion. A barbaric religion is one where the gods, not Man, are secondary, who have to be placated to avoid a curse, bribed to encourage fertility and the growth of crops, who are worshipped through fear or petition, not devotion. A barbaric religion is never proselytizing, it never seeks converts. An approximate distinction can be drawn between barbaric religions and those of "high cultures," as in the former the gods serve Man whereas in the latter Man serves the gods.

It may be objected by the eugenicist that there are many examples around the world where people do have their lives filled with religion without them contributing significantly to the cultural history of mankind, and that where cultural innovations are inspired by noble Causes this would not be possible without a sound genetic base in the first place. First, it is not true that intellect is required for sincere belief, and may actually be an impediment to it, so where we find sincere belief we do not *have* to find great cultural and technical innovation. The thesis here is not that social ideology *alone* is the begetter of great societies. In fact, after their age of irreligion "high cultures" return to mysticism and again under religious ages religions can actually be a cause of social stagnation when they become hierarchical and coercive, and like their embodying societies can endure for centuries unless destroyed. Decadence is a class phenomenon, affecting the intelligentsia who shrug off old belief while having the means to self indulge. As we see today, it is the upper classes that breed more slowly, college educated, professional women having the fewest children, while the poor are state supported and free to breed. The "high culture" is therefore encumbered not only with the loss of its former motivating ideology, it is also encumbered by a diminishing intelligentsia, due to decadence, combined with growing numbers of the mediocre who have no trouble adhering to mystical beliefs. With increasing economic problems that people feel they have no control over, mysticism deepens, but with a diminished intelligentsia the "high culture" is nothing more than a shell of its former glory.

Secondly, high population caliber in no way guarantees that people will automatically be devoted servants of a great ideal. The boat building and warrior skills of the Vikings and their courage in crossing stormy seas testify to the worthy caliber of those ancient people, yet their court consisted of nightly drinking bouts. One king, Fjolnier, drowned in a vat of mead. It is often assumed that the Mongol Empire was won by massive onslaughts; in reality the Mongol warriors were at times outnumbered by those they vanquished. Regardless of acumen, in both cases neither Viking nor Mongol produced a growing, organic society of their own, here termed a "high culture," but instead succumbed to the social organisms they invaded. Unlike the Puritans with Christianity, or the Arabs with Islam, what both Viking and Mongol lacked was a life purpose devotion, except possibly to war.

In presenting the above motivational explanation for the rise and fall of civilization it is not the intention to negate the obvious importance of environmental and eugenic factors. An indigenous technologically advanced civilization is unlikely among the Inuit, as it is among the Sahara Bedouin, for reason of their discouraging environments; and equally true is the claim of eugenicists for the need of substantial numbers of constitutionally and intellectually sound people within a population. The trouble with both environmental and eugenic explanations is that, emphasizing solely the *ability* of populations to rise and prosper, they are premised on the notion that given such ability populations must indeed rise and prosper. No such premise can be automatically established. Ability is a necessary condition, of course, but it is not a sufficient condition. Furthermore, a viable theory is required not only to explain the rise and fall of "high cultures," it has to explain their pattern of development, i.e., the massive expenditure of energy on nonutilitarian works during their early stages in contrast to later periods when emphasis on utilitarianism is actually the prelude to decline. This reversed character of the "high culture" cycle does not make sense if civilization were simply the result of people's struggle for animal existence.

But just as religion influences social development, so do social environment and intelligence impact on religious beliefs. As society matures we can expect religion to become less ethereal with less emphasis on gods and art and more concerned with the down-to-Earth affairs of an increasingly confident population. Thus the metamorphosis of a "high culture" when it changes into the second half of its life cycle and its more mundane, people-oriented 'Roman' stage of practical works. And as affluence and knowledge increase, when social ideology has no rational foundation, as myth religions rarely do, the feedback on that ideology must become a threat from the society's intellectual leaders and their influence on the populations of the entire "high culture".

If social ideology is crucial in the life of civilization, the loss of that inducement must also be significant. Looking at the "high culture" cycle, we in fact find that in each case the civilization declined after an age of irreligion and skepticism toward the old belief. Historians Spengler (The Decline of the West), Toynbee (A Study of History), Quigley (Tragedy and Hope), and de Riencourt (The Coming Caesars) have noted that the passing of great civilizations begins not with external degradation but with internal decay, serving as a warning to Western Civilization. Again in the words of Quigley:

>...there appears, for the first time, a moral and physical
>weakness which raises, also for the first time, questions
>about the civilization's ability to defend itself against ex-

ternal enemies. Racked by internal struggles of a social and constitutional character, weakened by loss of faith in its older ideologies and by the challenge of newer ideas incompatible with its past nature, the civilization grows steadily weaker until it is submerged by outside enemies, and eventually disappears.[13]

Conservative commentator and author, Patrick J. Buchanan, possibly said it best:

Is there a parallel between a dying Christianity in the West and the death of Japan's prewar and wartime faith? When nations lose their sense of mission, their mandate of heaven, the faith that brought them into this world as unique countries and cultures, is that when they die? Is that when civilizations perish? So it would seem.[14]

All "high cultures" have had profound influence upon intellectual development, evidenced from calendars, mathematics, writing, inventions and scientific inquiry. Not only are education and expanding knowledge the reasons, the city itself is a mental stimulus as it brings personal confidence and introduces more chance of easy transference of ideas than a rural community. This growing intellectual refinement and affluence of civilized people inevitably places them in conflict with the mystical and irrational beliefs of their forbearers. The most ardent 'Bible thumpers' today are hard pressed to rationalize their doctrine in the light of modern knowledge, the loss of faith in "older ideologies" (Christianity) by "the challenge of newer ideas" (evolution) has indeed weakened Western morale, and the same loss of faith was no less evident in

---

13 Carrol Quigley, *Tragedy and Hope*, pages 3 – 4.
14 *The Death of the West*, page 22

ancient societies once Nature's phenomena were understood to be natural events that could be predicted. In Greece, for example, the gods seemed banished from the sky by Thales predicting a solar eclipse and proclaiming that heavenly bodies moved in accordance with fixed laws. The Sophists openly took up the challenge of science and directly opposed belief in the gods, for which they often were driven from cities and had their books burned.

And so the period is reached, at some time or other in the life of a "high culture," when religion no longer possesses its former vitality. This loss does not occur in one generation, the new irreligion develops because of renewal of generations, when the older fails to arouse the younger with its own convictions. Since religion up to this point was so important to civilization it is reasonable to expect a crisis, and the first manifestation of devotional loss is its replacement with nationalism, a well-known phenomenon, an example occurring in the Canadian province of Quebec whose population for generations had been devoutly Catholic, but where, with infringement of the modern world, religion was replaced by the nationalist cause of separation from Canada. Although Israel is a nation founded by people who define themselves by religion, there is nothing surprising about a very high percentage of Israelis being atheist or agnostic, and that the majority of Jews in Israel never attend Synagogue on Saturday mornings. Their loss of religious enthusiasm may actually *enhance* their Zionism. The *founder* of modern Zionism, Theodor Herzl, was an atheist. On the scale of the entire "high culture" waning religious devotion transposes into virulent nationalism with consequent international rivalry and entire civilizations experiencing a period of fratricidal "world wars". The First and Second World Wars of the West were not without their predecessors in the Peloponnesian Wars of ancient Greece and similar catastrophes in other "high cultures". These bring into being the peripheral 'Roman' power already predisposed to the social and material requirements of the utilitarian age.

Of what consist the lives of people when they are deprived of their life purpose devotion? The one way that they can fill this vacuum is with themselves, so in contrast to an age when people were psychologically oriented with an ethical striving, after the fires of nationalism have burned out the undermining of religious sentiment leads to a new age when the search for 'happiness' becomes paramount. With the undermining of ideology people have no recourse but to fall on themselves for motivation, thereby changing the "high culture" from one of great music, painting, philosophy, ideas, that in large measure were inspired by the old ideology, to one of pragmatism and concern for the masses. Everything becomes geared for *use* by people, to promote their 'happiness'. Endeavor then must be justified by utilization, for the average citizen does not require fine art and philosophy. Roads and material enjoyment are of more vital concern. Cultural innovation of centuries combined with desires and intelligence impel a vast expansion of trade, fabulous feats of engineering and an increase in wealth. Outwardly people become sophisticated, inwardly they become egoists, but as egoists they differ from barbarians only in their domesticated tameness, resulting from a refined mode of living.

From there it is simply a question of time to the more blatant manifestations of social decadence. It is this, the people centeredness of a 'modern' world, that underlies the slide from discipline to permissiveness, from thrift to ostentatious materialism, from morality to sensuality, from the sublime in the arts to the exotic and erotic, from defense to pacifism, from nationalism to universalism, and the entire gamut of examples from striving to degeneration. Because humanism, pacifism, equalitarianism, liberalism, communism, universalism all stem from the same people-centeredness of a civilization that has lost its soul, they can all be classified, from the point of view of history, as decadent ideals. Decadence may even include the dysgenic rot of the populace, since with the establishment of a mass society selective forces are eliminated, and in combination with the materialist, hedonist sterility of propertied classes the whole tendency is then to balance numbers in favor of mediocrity.

This view of religion playing a pivotal role in the life of a "high culture" may seem to be contradicted in the case of China, because the Chinese, although superstitious are not a religious people. Actually, China is no contradiction at all since that civilization has been endowed with Confucianism, which is a *secular* religion that for centuries was taught by the state. Like all civilizations, China began in a Feudal Age, originally comprised of many states situated on the Yellow River. At this period many gods were worshipped as well as ancestors. By 1100 BC the Chinese were also worshipping a natural force, T'ien, translated as "Heaven," that ruled all other gods. It was believed that emperors could only rule while they had the "Mandate of Heaven," and this belief was held throughout Chinese history until Communism.

Following a period of "Warring States," 403 - 221BC, China became united under Emperor Shih Hwangti, 221 - 206 BC, which was the beginning of the Chinese Empire that has endured and expanded over two millennia to eventually become modern China, the longest lasting political entity in history. Its analogy in the West would be as if the Roman Empire never ended, but absorbed its invaders. It is on this long legacy that the Chinese people base a sense of mutual belonging, and also a sense of superiority. The reason for the difference between China and ancient Rome is the Confucian ethic of order and obedience that fuelled Chinese history since the beginning of the Han dynasty, 206 BC - 220 AD. Other religions had influence in China too, notably Buddhism, which dealt with the afterlife, and Taoism that dealt with one's well being, but Confucianism guided the social realm that included government, relationships among levels of society, ethical guidelines for maintaining social order, education and family life. Central to Confucianism is the importance of the family, emphasizing respect children show to their parents, the high regard given elders that transfers to lawful authority figures, and an appreciation for learning, protocol and ceremony. Confucian practice became the characteristic world view of the Chinese and with it by extension the sense of belonging to a society and state, hence giving cohesion and collectivism to Chinese society. The authority of the Chinese state derives from it being regarded as the protector and embodiment of Chinese civilization. China is a civilization state more than a nation state. Whereas in the West people see the state as a necessary evil, to be challenged by civil authority, media or church, in China the state has been seen as an integral part of life, whose directors derived their right to govern from the ethical principles of Confucianism, with those directors tested for centuries in Confucian principles by an imperial examination system. Here is a lesson for all secular religions aspiring to be the underpinning of lasting civilization.

Confucianism, like all traditional religion, is not premised on an analytical understanding of the world. Confucius was more of a historian than a philosopher and his ethics were a codification of what gave the better functioning states in the past, so that when a dynasty became prosperous there was no divine proscription against abusive use of wealth and privilege, except that the "Mandate of Heaven" could be withdrawn but this applied to the ruler. China therefore has had periods of dynastic decline, the last being its "century of humiliation" when large parts became enclaves of Western nations and Japan. The Chinese were aware of the cycles in their history and divided each dynasty into four periods: Warrior, Intellectual, Merchant and Chaos. The Warrior Period was beset by constant battles between warlords attempting to establish dominance. Eventually the country would be united under one, and this ushered in a period of art, invention and learning to give the Intellectual Period. Then the Merchants took over, which led to corruption and exploitation of the people, then finally to collapse in the period of Chaos. That would lead to the end of the dynasty and then the Warrior Period again. The Chinese sages tried to warn their emperors of the pattern who would never listen and Chinese history repeated itself. Most interesting is how people would try to protect themselves in the period of Chaos: it was always by *monasteries.* The same happened in the West after the collapse of Rome.

Again we might ask, if all "high cultures" have generally followed a similar pattern of development due to phasing through similar patterns in religious adherence, ending in what historians have called a 'Universal Empire' or 'world' government that gave peace and free trade to their known 'worlds', where is the Western 'Rome'? Surely by the time of our modern age of decline the West would have had time to see some development towards that establishment. Indeed we should, and do with the United Nations, military alliances and trading blocs, but no all-conquering military empire, and the reason for that absence is that the one and only candidate for the 'empire' distinction, the United States, originated from European colonialism. The U.S. did not grow from a feudal society as did Europe and all other "high cultures". The Feudal Age in Europe was one where everyone knew his/her place within a religious framework, with the result that an overall, collective perception of society as an organic whole prevailed. This was the soil from which grew the nations of Europe. When seventeenth century liberalism came into vogue, which emphasized the individual, this organic perception in Europe was not lost. A synthesis between old and new emerged that could produce movements like Socialism. Colonies spun off from Europe before the liberal revolution, in Quebec and Latin America, maintained the collective outlook, but colonies founded after that revolution, in the United States, Australia and English Canada, were peopled with liberal settlers who shrugged off the old organic view. Thus we see nationalism in these countries identified with individual benefit, such as America being the champion of private enterprise and a repository of rights and freedoms for all people. When the American national origins policy in immigration was scrapped in 1965, President Lyndon Johnson proclaimed that policy "un-American". In World War II the English, French, Russians, Germans and Japanese fought for England, France, Russia, Germany and Japan, but Americans fought for "freedom". When Quebec separatists expressed their desire for a sovereign Quebec to protect their unique national culture, English Canadians could only ask: "What does Quebec want?" With a country founded on individual rights and freedoms colonialism to Americans has always been an embarrassment, and a conquering military empire has been impossible even when in the pragmatic interest of peace and prosperity for all, including the conquered. In the case of America we have an example of how cycles in history can be, if not exactly broken, at least modified. We are not prisoners of our collective past.

If, on the other hand, religion is of no importance to the maintenance of a civilization, we have to ask about the Islamic world, which suffered deadly assaults from Mongols in the East, the loss of Spain in the West and later European colonialism over all, yet remained intact as a civilization. That was because the Islamic world maintained its religion and therefore its social cohesion, even its rift between Suni and Shia did not affect *belief*, unlike the Classical world that tolerated all religions, for which Christianity can be thankful, but whose own Olympian gods were replaced by Greek Stoicism and Epicureanism among its educated, Eastern cults among its poor and indifference generally. Classical Civilization was erased, and so would have been Islamic Civilization except that learning in the Islamic world has always had a symbiotic relationship with religious instruction centered in the *kutt'b* system, consisting of schools taught by the faithful in mosques, private homes, shops, tents and even out of doors. Originally Islamic scholarship flourished with an impressive openness to the rational sciences, art and literature, that produced outstanding contributions in chemistry, botany, medicine, physics, mineralogy, mathematics, astronomy and social philosophy. But as inevitable conflict between rationality and mythology developed, it would not be difficult in such a system to favor mythology. After the twelfth century Islamic learning was replaced by memorization of the Koran with little attempt made to analyze or discuss the meaning of the text, and a limited range of instructed subjects. The Islamic world survived, but at the cost of stagnation. The same was true of the Catholic world after the Reformation, where teaching of Church dogma became more enforced with the Counter Reformation and establishment of the Jesuit order, causing consequent decline of Catholic Europe compared to the North where, especially in Germany, secular schools were established after the Reformation. The danger of parochial education is no less evident today, when in America fundamentalist Christian organizations attempt to influence schoolbooks teaching evolution.

VI

The future outcome of the Cosmic Imperative expressed as a living entity will be realized through religious adherence, and that collectivity will be seen as a civilization. Because of its foundation in science and rational thought, and the penchant of humanity toward a better life brought by science and rational thought, the direction of world religion in the future is evident: a rational religion will one day be the guiding belief of all peoples. All humanity is destined to accept a religion of enlightenment, and a world religion implies a world civilization. Since we know the end development of all "high cultures" has been an all-encompassing 'world' empire, as was the Roman Empire for the Classical world, we have the implication that a world civilization will eventually be headed by an all-encompassing government. Those past civilizations declined because their founding religions were mythical and irrational, further implying that one based on rational knowledge in an enlightened age will give a civilization without decadence and disappearance. When social ideology is based on myth and mysticism, decadence is inevitable, because with the increasing affluence and knowledge that civilization brings, the old myths are eventually questioned. Authors Rodney Stark and William Bainbridge, in *The Future of Religion* (page 456), state that *... faiths in the future will contain no magic, only religion....* On that we can readily agree.

Religion can be defined as *a belief system characterized by the hope of salvation through fidelity to the belief.* There must be hope but there must also be loyalty; we cannot be both Christian and Moslem at the same time, and through that loyalty the believer gains 'salvation'. Nothing in this definition tells us religion must only be about the mystical. To be noted is that it has no reference to *God* or any spiritualism. A political movement can have religious implication too by this definition, as did National Socialism based on the hope of an Aryan world, and Communism with its promise of a "workers' paradise". Essential for that hope is loyalty to the belief, so in their promises of a better world both Communism and National Socialism can be considered *secular* religions. Atheistic Humanism is another, which offers the hope of a better world brought by an evolved humanity, and in this sense so is *Cosmos Theology,* only given the *Cosmic Imperative* its hope for the future can be offered with more certainty. Knowledge of Life's inevitable advancement alone cannot inspire hope and loyalty, but coupled to a political world order its enlightenment constitutes a secular belief the same as Humanism and mass political movements. By first knowing and following its Path we bring ourselves into harmony with the future of Life. It is the hope of Higher Man, a hope offered by belief confirmed with the certainty of our evolutionary past.

Establishment of a world civilization will require a type of Emergent World Order (EWO) different from the 'world' empires of the past, as it will be one that will embrace all humanity, and with control over humanity comes a responsibility for more than merely the regulation of society. With it government will have control over the destiny of Man for all time. That suggests the need for an

EWO to be a conscious agent of the *Cosmic Imperative*, which in turn means that in addition to being a regulative body it must also function as a *religious* institution. Having control over the destiny of Man without ideological enlightenment would mean no destiny at all, since Man would surely degenerate as we see in the decay of civilizations when they lose their engendering religions. Human beings are still heavily motivated by their animal past. We need philosophical direction for advancement along the Cosmic Path. That need for a religious motif to an EWO derives from its need to inspire civilization, including in an age of enlightened learning, so we come to a second realization in that its religion cannot be one typical of traditional religion, i.e., based on myth and mysticism. If it is to fulfill its mandate as a civilizing influence its expounded ideology in an enlightened world must have rational support. This, of course, is the claim of *Cosmos Theology*, making it the natural theology of an EWO. In that day we can expect humanity to have a world order giving it the unity of a common religious belief, one that is not limited to addressing what have been the normal concerns of government, namely: to maintain peace, provide laws with enforcement for the protection of individuals and regulation of commerce, to provide services and aid for the economically distressed. A government limited to these functions alone has no control over the ultimate destiny of the society it encompasses, that is, over the more basic, human forces propelling civilization.

The modern West has been thoroughly indoctrinated with the notion that Church and State should be separate, but all civilizations have begun and grown in periods when the temple was virtually inseparable from rule. It is the divorcement of social ideology from the common affairs of life that undermines the structural strength of society, ultimately ending in its collapse. Opposition to religion in modern politics is owing to religions being of traditional, mythological form, whose doctrines were obtained by divine revelation. Of course it would be absurd, and dangerous, to have any such religion embraced by government, or any government embraced by such religion, because all were forged in ignorant and credulous periods and have continued to reflect that genesis. When belief cannot be supported by reason it must be supported by coercion. This would less likely apply to a rational philosophy, presentable on better grounds than narrow and subjective dogma.

Apart from how rational a philosophy may be, the fear of combining Church and State is also due to the nature of moral law: it is authoritative. The Church is not prone to formulate policies on the basis of popular concern, nor does the Vatican College of Cardinals pick a pope by popular vote among the world's population of Roman Catholics. The Ten Commandments were not determined by voting. It cannot be otherwise with moral philosophy, for although people choose the doctrine they are to practice, doctrine itself is either revealed by the divine or promulgated by examination and understanding, and cannot be subject to public whim. We cannot have moral principles determined by voting and forever expect those principles to be moral. We know from entropic regression that they would degenerate. Laws derived from doctrine are therefore authoritative, and so must be the organization that imposes them. It may be thought in the modern world that the Church ultimately does follow the mores of its community, as in the case of the Church of England's 1992 change of policy to allow women to be ordained priestesses, or the liberalization of Communion for divorced and remarried Catholics in Germany although such marriage is strictly forbidden by Scripture (Matt. 19: 9). Examples like these only demonstrate the conflict of Church policies with reason in an enlightened age, and are the kind of examples that show the need for rationality in social philosophy.

Moral philosophy gives structure to society, and to cast responsibility for its implementation to the vagaries of public conscience is to submit humanity to the same threat of social decadence that has brought all past civilizations to dust. The issue revolves on the nature of the two major types of law required for any society: regulative and imperative, where the regulative is usually derived from the imperative. Regulative law is the type we associate with democratic assemblies, arrived at by voting, and includes laws governing such matters as commerce and licensing. The distinction between the two types of law can be seen in the game of baseball:

Every baseball player knows that with three strikes the batter is 'out'. There may be differences of opinion between the players on whether a particular pitch constituted a strike, or on any play, so for a smoother game an umpire is selected. The umpire applies the rules but does not make them, neither do the players. The umpire is a *regulative* authority, and owing to that function it would be wise if each team had a voice in his/her selection, the selection made on the basis of knowledge of the game and impartiality to each side. This need for control over regulators by participants is inherent in the nature of regulative authority. But every player submits to the rules, without questioning them or devising new rules before each game, to decide, say, if a batter should be allowed four strikes instead of three. The rules themselves have been laid down by custom, and because those rules must be followed to have the game of baseball, on which there is no voting, the authority of custom regarding the players is something more than just regulative. Of course, the players could pick another game to play, like soccer, but once they choose they must submit to the rules. If a player does not submit and breaks those rules, he/she acts *immorally*.

Imperative laws have differed remarkably between societies, and in every case they have been so ingrained in the public conscience that a society without them was thought impossible or intolerable. We know from a list of examples (pages 34-36) how moral perceptions can differ between peoples. The Soviet Union was another case, one where government framed policies within Marxist-Leninism, and the practice of that economic system was elevated to moral status. Capitalism has been morally conjoined to the principle of individual liberty. The Cold War demonstrated with its threat of nuclear annihilation how fiercely moral principles can be held, and although the people of a society esteem them right, just and natural, they are learned. Such is the nature of social philosophy and religion; where it is accepted its teachings become internalized to the degree that perceptions are molded and people are motivated from within rather than by decree or legislation. Where this is not the case, we have modern Western society where morally ambiguous problems involve legalized drugs, same sex marriages, abortion, prostitution, euthanasia and gambling, which remain largely unresolved. These questions cannot be satisfactorily answered in modern society because there is no real authority outside the Church to appeal to, and when an appeal is made to that authority the reply is premised on dogmatic narrowness that cannot hold respect. The most heated controversies are generated over these concerns when legislated upon in democratic assemblies, and laws passed are generally unsatisfactory, sometimes temporary, because moral problems cannot be resolved by majorities, belonging as they do under imperative law. When the authority of that law breaks down, society is thrown into confusion.

Evident is that any social enterprise, from a game of baseball to the total collective of society as a whole, proceeds from a set of rules that may be unstated, upon which there is no voting, and which are imposed either by Nature, custom, economics or by an institution, but imposed in a way that they are internalized by the individual. Regulative law controls action, imperative law controls thought. People can refuse to accept these rules but once accepted all authority over them is surrendered. If an institution imposes them by indoctrination, that institution is authoritative. Society, like all creative endeavors, requires structure for its endurance, and it is this adherence to rules that gives such structure, regardless of the freedoms exercised by people. If a major responsibility of government is to be the continued evolution of Man and society along the Path of the *Cosmic Imperative*, it must have a means of such imperative rule making, and like any philosophical institution the means employed must also be authoritative. Care, however, should be taken not to confuse absolutism with totalitarianism. The Soviet Union under the Communist Party was totalitarian, being in total control of Soviet society, whereas the Catholic Church is absolutist on matters of moral belief, yet Catholic countries, such as France, can obviously be free and democratic. It is in this latter sense that absolutism is advocated, which is not a contradiction to the need and desire for democracy in the everyday ruling of nations. Democracy is the only form of government that is directly accountable to the people it governs, and therefore regarded as the only legitimate form of government. At the same time a world order cannot ignore the lesson of history that social ideology and its institutions are of vital importance to a growing society, which in turn leads to a realization for the need of imperative authority. The conclusion is paradoxical, but there is no escaping it.

For an enduring civilization on the Path of Life two branches of government must be in place due to the divide between regulative and imperative law: democratic assemblies representing regulative authority where would reside actual power and control, and a body providing ideological directorship, to achieve in government the balance between order and freedom required for a dynamic society. We can imagine that the seat of regulative authority would require an Assembly of Nations analogous to the General Assembly of the United Nations, which would be the seat of actual power. Here would sit representatives from all the world's nations, and all would need guaranteed democratically elected national governments. A Prime Minister would be elected by these representatives who would be the executive power of the EWO, and in this regard the Assembly would have a Parliamentary system, reflective of the United Nations. The Prime Minister could therefore be deposed if not satisfying the will of the majority, and have less of a god-like stature than if he/she were elected by the world's citizens.

Up to this point we can speculate that an EWO government would reflect the organization of our present United Nations, but the demands of the future would require much more. For one, the guarantee of democracy would be one imposition of the EWO on the more autocratic nations of the world, and that would include universal suffrage. Surveillance and extirpation of national corruption would be another. A contentious imposition on nations would be the denial of a national military to any nation. There would be only one military, and that would be under the Assembly of Nations; there would be no national militaries. International war would therefore be impossible. Another imposition would be loss of total control of national governments over their school systems. The full development of the human being, including critical thinking, is the religious mission obliged by the Cosmic Imperative but is not necessarily in any national interest, as compared to, for instance, technological or business instruction. Different ideologies could be taught, but with examination and criticism, and this would include *Cosmos Theology*. But technological subjects, the arts or any subjects crucial to a nation's economy would be under national jurisdiction. One imposition that would likely not be imposed is a market union. Although an international currency issued by the EWO would facilitate trade and travel, the history of the European Union has shown that complete monetary and labor integration between economies as diverse as those of Greece and Germany is more idealistic than practical. The EWO would wisely *not* impose any such integration. Other than the impositions mentioned, the EWO by its ideological constitution would not restrict national sovereignty, national or racial expressions or in any way seek to diminish world diversity. On the contrary, it would work to increase the number of nations represented in its Assembly of Nations, and this would be at the expense of multicultural imperial states now in existence. In effect, the EWO would need to be a *federation* rather than a world state. With most political functions presently in the possession of sovereign states remaining with sovereign states, including immigration and currency, it would be a looser federation than the present European Union.

Even under an absolutist government, in devising and executing domestic social and economic policies, and in enforcing the laws of its legislature, a democratic regime must operate, but the natural question is: if an enduring civilization is to evolve, the expectation is that its ideological institutions would represent progress in human thought, and what institutions in the modern world could be embryonic in giving moral direction? Traditionally in the West this has been the Church, but for a rational philosophy we might acknowledge the institutions that are already recognized as the apex of rational thought: the *universities*. Not only are they seats of learning, they are also seats of expertise that today influences state policies in multitudinous ways, and universities also influence the minds of a nation's brightest youth, meaning that they are already seats of imperative authority. To extend that authority to ethics is not excessively speculative. If the educational system became a totally integrated system from beginning years to the highest awards of university, a system would be in place to solicit the type of life purpose allegiance characterizing civilization. The result would be a civilization dedicated not to mythical and mystical fantasies, nor to business or sport or the various pleasures of a decadent culture. Nor would it be a civilization devoted to Man in the humanist sense, but instead to the flowering of human potential. Its education system would be the originator of imperative law, decreed from what might be termed an *Imperative Council* composed of the most gifted minds that nations have to offer, selected, not elected, through the ranks of their education systems. Instead of decrees from notions of infallibility derived from heaven, the decrees of an 'Imperative Council' would be propounded with mathematical assurance.

Most governments are composed of two houses and the EWO would be no different, the second house being a combination of church, supreme court and university. Here would be seated the *imperative* side of law whose members would be *selected* up through the world's education systems. This 'Imperative Council' would be the apex of the world's education systems. Whereas the Assembly of Nations would be a democracy, the 'Imperative Council' would be a meritocracy, headed by a President. Not being a body of representatives it could have no agency power, its authority derived purely from its expertise and ability to persuade, and that by means of education and the world's propaganda systems. Knowledge is power and this would be the preserve of the 'Imperative Council'. In addition, this council would also be the seat of ideology, one substantiated by actual knowledge instead of the myth and mysticism of traditional religion, thereby fulfilling its global responsibility for enduring human progress, even evolution. In this fulfillment an EWO government would differentiate itself from the decadent imperial rule normally associated with an aging civilization. Its ideology would be the ideology of the Cosmos taught in its school systems, and although any and all desired religions would also be taught, and critically examined, we can foresee that one in agreement with rationality and adapted to the realities of science would be advantaged, to advance to the highest positions in the world's school systems. The most learned practitioners of this ideology would form the pool from which members of the 'Imperative Council' would be drawn. By this means the leading body of the EWO would be essentially a religious order.

In a rationalist world science and religion will not be separate. Once rational knowledge is brought into a religious outlook both will be taught as one, as was always meant to be, in the spirit of Medieval colleges. As with any government, the coming world government will divide between regulative and imperative authority, only in its case it will *knowingly* do so. Although humanity has followed many codes in the past, the objective of its imperative division will be to determine and encourage what codes humanity *should* follow for compliance with the Cosmic Path. Therefore, in addition to being a religious body the 'Imperative Council' will be the culminating head of the world's education systems. Here will reside philosophical directorship, which together with a democratic Assembly of Nations will achieve in world government the dynamic balance between order and freedom required for human advancement. Its philosophy will disclose the Mission of all who follow the Path of Life as participation in the Ultimate Destiny of Life, and explain the pathos of evil, which in essence is the pathos of failure – failure to trod on the road of Creation. The result will be a paradise world not unlike the mystical prophecies described in the Bible. Consider Isaiah 35: 5 - *Then shall the eyes of the blind be opened, and the ears of the deaf unstopped. Than shall the lame man leap like a deer, and the tongue of the dumb shall sing,. . .* These marvels will indeed occur, not by mystical belief but in a rational world of learning. In that day we can realistically expect a world free from suffering, the end of poverty, extended longevity embracing centuries and the complete control of natural forces in a world governed by the intelligence of a civilization beyond imagining.

Having no agency power, it may be thought that an

'Imperative Council' would be an academic body only, but care should be taken in this assessment. Imperative authority is not lacking in modern society and has been revealed in books blatantly describing it as such. One of the first was simply titled "Propaganda," 1928, by Edward Bernays, a nephew of Sigmund Freud, who was an influential figure in the US Committee on Public Relations, and as propagandist had CBS, American Tobacco Company, General Electric and the United Fruit Company numbered among his clients. Bernays begins his book with:

> The conscious and intelligent manipulation of the organized habits and opinions of the masses is an important element in democratic society. Those who manipulate the unseen mechanism of society constitute an invisible government which is the true ruling power of our country.
>
> We are governed, our minds molded, our tastes formed, our ideas suggested, largely by men we have never heard of. This is a logical result of the way in which our democratic society is organized . . .
>
> They govern us by their qualities of natural leadership, their ability to supply needed ideas and by their key position in the social structure. Whatever attitude one chooses toward this condition, it remains a fact that in almost every act of our daily lives, whether in the sphere of politics or business, in our social conduct or our ethical thinking, we are dominated by the relatively small number of persons . . . It is they who pull the wires which control the public mind, who harness old social forces and contrive new ways to bind and guide the world.[15]

---

15. Bernays, Propaganda, pages 37-38

With Enlightenment a time of 'people power' actually was achieved, but Bernays continues:

> *Today, however, a reaction has set in. The minority has discovered a powerful help in influencing majorities. It has been found possible so to mold the mind of the masses that they will throw their newly gained strength in the desired direction. In the present structure of society, this practice is inevitable. Whatever of social importance is done today, whether in politics, finance, manufacture, agriculture, charity, education, or other fields, must be done with the help of propaganda. Propaganda is the executive arm of the invisible government.[16]*

Such persuasion should not be taken lightly in its ability to mold society, for a look at the world as it is today reveals that the political revelation of Edward Bernays was hardly due to imagination. Most Americans, for example, believe that something as fundamental in their lives as money is created by a government agency, whereas in reality it is created through debt by a consortium of private banks, the Federal Reserve, the same as European "national" banks are private banks on which shares are sold. This ignorance takes a toll on American national wealth because it is from the sale of bonds, that is, from borrowing, that the federal government receives its financing, on which it pays interest, in effect meaning that the country pays interest on its own money. This cost is unnecessary because government financing could be done directly from the Treasury and subtracted from the money system by tax-

---

16 Bernays, Propaganda, pages 47-48

ation without that interest burden, but this fact will not be found in any college text on economics. Instead, private bank financing of public works is justified as a system in league with free enterprise. Another example of psychological conditioning is of the feminist movement in America that has generally raised the level of consciousness for the need of equality between the sexes, even to the point of changing the English language[17]. Again, nothing would seem more fundamental to a nation than its national character, yet the opinions of Americans and Canadians have been conditioned in schools and media to accept liberal multiculturalism as de facto national policy. No election or referendum has ever been held in the United States or Canada on a policy so inimical to the ethnicity of White nations, yet accepted it has been, and this through the machinery of persuasion. Let not the critics of an 'Imperative Council' argue that present society is free from the reins of imperative control.

Bernays is content to leave this power of persuasion to the mandarins of business, without acknowledging that they too might be influenced by social decadence. Far better to have the authoritative power of persuasion wielded by a philosophically superior elite aware of the laws of the Universe. One should not think that imperative authority necessarily means the suppression of individual thought. On the contrary, since the Cosmic Imperative compels human progress, and the only way to have human progress is by having freedom and education, meaning above all

---

17 As in changing words like "chairman" to "chair*person*" even though 'wo*man*' ends with the suffix. 'Woman' probably means 'man with a womb.' The term 'Man' is generic. Changes in the English language like this are linguistically pointless, and in any case – is not 'per*son*' equally "sexist"?

freedom of thought, an 'Imperative Council' could not by its mandate be an ideologically oppressive body.

This subliminal influence of an 'Imperative Council' is a necessary feature of that council, owing to human weakness that inevitably tends toward *entropic regression* but often not recognized as such, that we see in the liberalization of opinions and practices in the guise of "progressive" human interest. These are easily accepted by the public, especially when promoted as "politically correct," that is, when presented as the obvious choice of people when not influenced by ideological bias. But a religion of the Cosmos does present an ideological bias, that of the *Cosmic Imperative*, often entailing *struggle* rather than "happiness." The EWO, to be a true Creative agent of the *Cosmic Imperative*, cannot be another mere instrument of humanity, like the United Nations, regardless of the well intentioned premises of the latter. The end of war and supply of provisions to needy nations are, of course, a part of that imperative, which concern the present but not the future in an evolutionary sense, because the evolution of any species invariably entails struggle, and that is not on any U. N. agenda that by its mandate must concern itself with human welfare and "happiness."

An example would be the question of race and racial hybridization. Let no one believe this envisioned EWO suggests the liberal multiculturalism of a decadent civilization. The diversity brought by the intermingling of many peoples is a temporary illusion, and a mass intermingling of peoples is not necessary for the benefit of cultural innovations introduced from around the world, often given as the justification for multiculturalism. Europeans themselves made the introduction of oriental advancements into Medieval Europe, whether as Crusaders or travellers such as the Polos. The heavy presence of Western influence in Japan does not require millions of White faces in that nation. On the contrary, there is evidence from history that multiculturalism is destructive of great societies. No society could have been more multicultural (or cosmopolitan, as it was then called) than that of *decadent* Rome. Rome was the world government of its time, and in its streets were races and peoples from every part of its empire. Reflecting upon the fate of the Roman Empire, it would be untruthful to say that multiculturalism was of any lasting benefit to that great world, and naïve to assert it as an inspiration for future human progress (see Appendix A).

We must further wonder whether a racially mixed society is conducive to the *Cosmic Imperative* from that concept implying a well-integrated community leading through self-organization and emergence to a higher level of complexity. Obviously for that to happen there is the requirement of maximum harmony and trust, but the findings of one study, published in 2007 on diversity and trust within communities, conducted on 30,000 people in the United States, were so disturbing to its author, Robert Putnam, that he delayed publishing them six years from the time of his research in 2001. The study found that low trust with high ethnic diversity is associated with lower confidence in local government, local leaders and local news media, lower confidence in one's own influence, lower frequency of registering to vote, less expectation that others will cooperate to solve dilemmas of collective action, less likelihood of working on a community project, less likelihood of giving to charity or volunteering, fewer close friends and confidants, less happiness and lower perceived quality of life, and more time spent watching television. Most disturbing was the finding that diversity not only causes less trust between ethnic groups, it also causes less trust *within* ethnic groups. Clearly a harmonious community is not served by multiculturalism. With the example of Rome in mind, we might see it as an expression of social dissolution, undoubtedly the most egregious the Western world is experiencing today. That Putnam made his discovery should not be surprising to anyone familiar with entropic regression, since multiculturalism is the setting for racial amalgamation that *in time* gives homogeneity, not diversity.

Instead, the world of the future when the Cosmic Imperative is followed will be a world where racial and national differences are respected. Complexity dictates diversity, as with our bodies that are not homogenous cellular masses but composed of different organs. We can expect the same of a viable Emergent World Order. The laws of Nature apply on all scales, whether in the formation of the first multicellular life or in the organization of living forms that now dominate the planet. All follow the same laws, which we ignore to our detriment, and the laws of Life dictate diversity and complexity on the global scale, not uniformity.

Life's diversification has an importance in Nature, and is indeed an exigency of the Cosmic Imperative. An essential ingredient of evolution by natural selection is death. About 99.9% of all species that ever existed on planet Earth are now dead. In their place we have evolutionarily advanced species. How does Nature "know" which species should live and which should die? Of course, Nature is not sentient and does not know. The species themselves decide through the trials of life with its competition, the less viable becoming extinct. To have this natural selection there has to be multitudes of species, which means diversity. The

Cosmic Imperative, the advancement of Life, demands it.

Human beings are not divorced from this natural demand of Nature, and as the latest phase transition in the long history of Life we should see the same trend toward diversification. That is what we see in the appearance of different races with their different cultures. We may be persuaded against this view by the fact that races are not species and can still interbreed with each other, which is an ability not permitted to different species without giving sterile hybrids, if they can interbreed at all. This ability of human races to interbreed should not blind us to the further fact that racial differentiation is the beginning stage of species differentiation. The reason for fertile human racial hybridization is the relatively short amount of time that human races have been separate - about 60,000 years - whereas roughly a half million years is required for sufficient genomic divergence producing different species. So the argument that human diversity is not an example of the Cosmic Imperative is false. With racial-cultural nationalism, desired by all peoples, we are complying with Cosmic Law, the essence of all morality.

But regardless of diversity, the world today is in need of the unity offered by a politically united planet. In our modern age we have world disparities worsened by exploitive policies of industrial nations and their gluttonous policies along with the self-fixated attitude of third world countries regarding economic development, both now causing environmental damage on a global scale. The world today has not only nuclear weapons but also their miniaturization, any one of which could be smuggled into a city of millions and detonated. Regional conflicts can threaten major war, and with the devastating power of modern weapons could threaten humanity. At the same time, the harmful economic effects of narrow nationalist policies are realized, encouraging open trade and understanding between nations. Technological innovation has made the world a smaller place with communications and travel, allowing people the world over to feel closer. The end result is the growing perception of a politically united world needed, one that must inevitably lead to a more united humanity than was ever possible within its fractious history. This world cannot forever remain politically disunited, and that need is becoming ever more perceived in the minds of the world's people. With another major war world political unity will be seen crucial to human safety and even survival.

Given the need there is no question that a politically united world will eventually transpire. As previously mentioned (page 56), 'world' governments existed before in the form of empires that gave 'world' peace and free trade that were the natural end stage of their civilizations, most of which decayed from within and were destroyed, the most notable being the Roman Empire. Western Civilization would be no different, except that we learned (pages 82-83) that the foremost power of the Western world, the United States, has not followed the usual pattern due to its genesis as a colony of Europe and therefore having a truncated psychological-sociological spectrum needed for the full development of a "high culture." In addition, Western decadence makes difficult any speculation on the required world order evolving from the West and lasting for any period of time.

The signs of a declining society are many and varied. These include: monopolization and concentrating economic power, exaggerated economic disparity, loss of manufacturing, externalization of elites (as with business globalization), inflation, increasing debt, concentrating political power with diminishing freedoms, rule of money, materialism, emboldenment of external enemies (as with radical Islamic movements), huge military expenditure, mass pacifism yet endemic wars, cosmopolitanism (multiculturalism), irreligion, growing irrationality, growing foreign beliefs, increasing mysticism, male effeteness, shrinking middle class, low birthrate, giant cities with shrinkage of the countryside population, hedonism, crass art, etc. All of these are evident in our modern West today. Most clearly, a major sign is a population's failure to reproduce itself, and this is evident with the founding population of the West. Over the decade 2000-2010, as reported by *The Economist*, March 2011, the American population grew by 9.7% to 309 million, with "minorities" comprising by far most of that growth. Hispanic and Asian populations grew 43% each and the Black by 11% while the White population only grew 1.2%, actually shrinking in California by 5% and in New Jersey and Rhode Island by 6%. "Minorities" are now majorities in California, Texas, New Mexico, Hawaii and Washington DC. "Minority" children are now majorities in Arizona, Florida, Georgia, Maryland, Mississippi and Nevada, indicating the next majority generations of those states. The number of White children fell in 46 states, overall by 10%. A similar story is evident in Western Europe relative to huge Moslem populations. If present fertility rates hold, Europe's population will decline to 207 million by the end of the twenty-first century, less than 30 percent of its present number.

If we think of civilization as a system, no system can survive when its components act individually. That is how Western people today act, think and feel, exclusively as individuals, from individual motivation with very little sense of belonging to any collective, especially their religious one. There is even the cult of the individual, which infers that there should be no imposition on individual rights, so that even a sordid pedophile can distribute his written fantasies if they possess a modicum of artistic expression. Whenever social trends destructive of Western nationhood are defended, they are always defended on the basis of individual rights. Whether in relaxed race relations, artistic license or "progressive" legislation, the motivation is always for increased individual freedom, expression and happiness. That is what people live for today in the West, not king or country, not God or Church, not for any idealism except ideals stemming from purely people concerns. Naturally, such a society will have an obsession with money. The tragedy of the Western world is that we are dissolving into a state of barbarism modified by domestic living. With their ring piercing, tattoos and freaky hairstyles, Western youths are even coming to look like barbarians. This fixation with the self easily extends to the family, because raising children means a sacrifice of time and wealth, a sacrifice deemed unnecessary when there is no sense of heritage. Many White families of means today would rather have a second car than a second baby, and some couples make a conscious decision to have no children.

Much has been written on environmental degradation being the cause of advanced cultures declining (e.g. *Collapse,* by Jared Diamond), an obvious possible factor that nonetheless overlooks the essence of civilization as an expression of our human proclivity to control the environment. One historian, Arnold Toynbee, even wrote of the human response to environmental challenge as the *cause* of civilization. The Mayan world may very well have fallen for lack or rain, but the entire Islamic world is not notable for its abundance of water. The essential reason for collapse is the loss of morale within the population, producing a loss of connectedness with the temporal society either of the present or past, and the major agent producing that connectedness has always been religion. There was a time when people of the West also were imbued with a sense of belonging and mission. America began not with buccaneers or wealthy capitalists but with Puritan settlers, and Europeans during the Middle Ages could travel from England to Italy and feel at home within an embracing Church. But few believe in an Immaculate Conception any more, or in religious miracles, or in personalized angels and demons, or in a personalized God that a man could wrestle with (Genesis 27: 30), or that evil came from a talking snake (Genesis 3: 1 - 4), or that woman came from man's rib (Genesis 21: 22), or that the Sun stood still in the sky to prolong the day (Joshua 10: 13), or that the Earth was created in six thousand years, or that lions will eat straw (Isaiah 11: 7) etc., so with the passing of religion we have what we have today: mass materialism and the "me" generation. Our present Western population is *decadent*. This has nothing to do with genetics; it is the result of people having nothing in their lives except their own lives. Instead of giant cathedrals we have giant shopping malls, and when people are most concerned with personal fulfillment they can empathize with all others who want the same. It is within this milieu that a philosophy of Life must spread, to secure a new civilization.

Thus, humanity has three scenarios for its future, each involving the unification of the globe under a world government, which is inevitable. The first two scenarios follow the usual course of history with the imposition of what has been termed by historians the "universal empire," like the

Roman, Persian, Inca, etc. that were the historical outcomes of their respective civilizations. Western Civilization is following this same course centred in the United States, and will decay the same as the others. Or the globe will succumb to the centuries old empire of China, whose imperial phase is most developed and proficient, always emphasizing unity and stability, being in existence for over two millennia during which it absorbed its invaders and underwent several periods of experimentation and adaptation, the latest being Communism. The old Confucian ethics of harmony, obedience, order, loyalty, ritual, emphasis on the collectivity rather than the individual, all combined with state supremacy, continued throughout the centuries. A glance at the territorial expansion of that empire over Asia since its inception in 206 BC gives an idea of one scenario that humanity may have in store for the immediate future (meaning centuries), beginning with a powerful world-wide hegemony after mid twenty-first century due to the remarkable growth of its economy. Alternatively, the third scenario is to have an enlightened Emergent World Order brought into existence by the struggle of people through religious conviction. Although the 'universal' empire is more certain in the short run, an Emergent World Order is the inevitable certainty in the long run because it embodies the *emergence* of humanity itself into a living form, and this is the Path of Life dictated by the *Cosmic Imperative*. There can be no higher stage of complexity for the human species, and this is the destiny intuited by moral philosophers. The imperial Roman-type 'world' state, on the other hand, instead of a unity of nations submerges nations and subjects into a formless humanity.

With the two scenarios for the short-range future involving 'world' empires like the Roman that are the usual development of their civilizations, we must ask: how do they figure in our evolutionary advancement? They did in the past but one in our global future does not. The decay of a global empire would hardly mean a phase transition in humanity's social or evolutionary development. The greatest worry about world government should therefore not be just about the loss of freedom; it should be about the decadence and decay of an imperial world state in which there will be the loss of freedom. Whether a future world empire is established by the United States or China, *neither* provides for another advancement of the *Cosmic Imperative*. On the contrary, the heavy military presence possessed by each will give no room or incentive for the *religious* component required for advancement to a higher order of civilization. Indeed, there will be religion, as in world empires myth and mysticism always reappear among the ruins of imperial decay, but not from any enlightened conception and therefore guaranteeing history's repeated cycling even if humanity ever again lifted itself up from our planet's environmental debasement. In addition, once a universal empire is established there is no reason to expect its corruption, injustice, poverty, exploitation and oppression to ever end. This was the case of China until its impact with the West, and with the lethal weaponry of the modern world a future empire will be even more firmly established. This is hardly the Path of Life.

Thus the difference between the world government envisioned by *Cosmos Theology* and one normally established by an imperial state is the recognition of the decadence that civilizations experience when not established on rational social ideology, and the provision of that rational ideology. The religions of past civilizations have been based in myth and superstition, that when examined in a progressive age are found false and therefore can no longer serve as the ideological requirement for their respective civilizations, which then collapse into atomized self-interest. The major tenet of *Cosmos Theology* is that our moral human duty is to serve the *Cosmic Imperative*, which is anathema to having humanity forever locked in the decadence and oppression of an imperial state. A world order has the religious *duty* of advancing humanity, not only materially but also morally, and therefore it must be more than just a *regulative* authority; it must also be a *religious* authority. Instead of separating Church and State, both must be as one in an enlightened global regime designed for perpetual human advancement without social decline.

The real question is not on the future development of a united world, that is inevitable, but on whether it will represent an *evolutionary* stage in human development. In contrast to a world government established from the pursuit of wealth, dominance and power, one established from an enlightened secular religion offers the only hope of a united Earth grounded in real world learning. A religion of the Cosmos is humanity's hope for the future, for it is the hope of a rational world propelling civilization itself into a higher order of Life, following Life's imperative of *emergence*. The major evolutionary requirement of the individual human agent is moral consciousness, for moral precepts are the requirement for total integration into that higher collectivity. These same moral precepts have become the preserve of religion, so we see how by giving beliefs in accordance with the Cosmic Path even traditional religion has prepared humanity for its collective future. What remains is to establish religious beliefs on substantive understanding for a lasting and *evolving* humanity and civilization.

18 There are exceptions, one being the hybridization of wolves and coyotes in the eastern U. S. and Canada that has produced a mixture better at coping with the reduced woodland brought by human settlement.

Appendix A

Multiculturalism –
Entropic Regression in the World Today:

A major controversial issue for modern Western nations raised by *Cosmos Theology* is the regressive quality of multi-culturalism. Only its social aspects have been treated, so we might ask: is that quality true on the more basic genetic level from the racial consequences of multiculturalism? That is, can we demonstrate a theoretical change in the incidence of unfavorable genetic combinations in a human population that undergoes racial mixture?

In plants and animals hybridization is usually a retar-dant to the adaptation process, producing less viable off-spring adapted to neither of the environments in which evolved the parent stocks. This accounts for the great diver-sity of species in the world. The need for environmental adaptation is a strict necessity, so that hybridization, partic-ularly in animals, leads to extinction[18], but in Man this con-sequence is not evident because the human species can, to a large extent, control the more drastic effects of its environ-ment. The disadvantages of hybridization in the case of human beings may appear to have been eliminated. What this conclusion fails to consider is that the success of human populations largely depends on an array of learned experi-

19 An example of how gene pairing gives an advantage is sickle cell anemia. If an individual has both genes for it he/she is debilitated, but only one gene in heterozygous pairing gives malaria resistance.

ences transmitted over the generations, summed up in the term *culture*, that it is an aptitude for learning cultural traits which is inherited, and that the furtherance of a population's culture to improve survival ability depends on the appearance of gifted persons. The adaptation of the animal that was transmitted directly through the genes has become in human beings an adaptation for learning, which in turn has genetic origins. Where and if such differences exist hybridization can disrupt this heredity, an occurrence that can be mathematically demonstrated.

Let us suppose a population where 400 out of 1000 people carry a gene required for any particular talent. This population accepts migrants from another population that differs in that frequency, the second population only averaging 70 people in 1000 with that gene. The mix will obviously contain a reduced number per 1000 than the original population. If migrants are in such number to constitute 20% of the new population, the new frequency will be 334 per 1000: a reduction of 16.5% from the original (calculations follow).

Any human ability is most likely the result of a combination of genes, so that the talent will not reveal itself unless an individual possesses a multitude of genes related to it. Let us assume that only one genetic pair promotes the mentioned talent, one gene inherited from each parent, and to keep things simple, the frequency of the second gene is the same in both populations, say, 100 people per 1000. Since two different genes in a pair are now required for an individual to possess the talent,[19] this now changes the frequency of the original population having that ability to 80 per 1000. If the two populations uniformly mix genetically, the frequency of talent in the mixed population changes to 67 per 1000, which reflects approximately the 16.5% reduction.

The appearance of any aptitude, however, is more realistically the result of multiple combinations involving a multitude of genes. Musical talent, for example, combined with a robust temperament may produce nothing, whereas combined with an effeminate temperament may produce a renowned performer. If the migrants also differ in these other qualities from the native population we can equally expect the frequency of talent to diminish.

Table 1:

Pop.	r	q	2qr	s	t	2st	2qr x 2st
Nat.	0.4	0.1	0.08	0.60	0.2	0.240	0.0192
Mig.	0.07	0.1	0.014	0.30	0.2	0.120	0.0017
Hyb.	0.334	0.1	0.0668	0.54	0.2	0.216	0.0144

In Table 1, columns r and q are the mentioned frequencies for our particular ability considered, columns s and t are those for any other characteristic required, such as temperament for musical performance, again simplistically assuming that one heterozygous pair is required for a unique quality. The last column shows the frequency of people likely gifted in the talent for the native, migrant and hybrid populations. Looking at the last column of Table 1, for a mix that is 20% migrant, the frequency of aptitude in the hybrid population, 14.4 people per 1000, is lower than the 19.2 people per 1000 of the unmixed native population. Translated into realistic quantities, in a population of 10 million the original population would have 192,000 gifted individuals, whereas the same population number mixed uniformly with the migrants would produce 144,000: a reduction. It is this cultural consequence of human hybridization, which bears no similarity to animal hybridization, that liberal geneticists and biologists have failed to recognize. Although the number of exceptionally talented people is small compared to the total population, it is nonetheless crucial because in any society it is the genius of the race that advances civilization. If this elite is diminished over the generations because of out-breeding from its racial genetic pool, the social, technical and general cultural achievements of that population will diminish.

Liberals who do not admit actual genetic differences between racial populations and the significance of the above treatment should consider the DRD4 gene. This is the so-called 'novelty' gene possessed by people who seek new experiences, associated with a high incidence of drug and alcohol addiction. Combined with various talents it has also been found associated with people described as "high-energy, self-confident adventurers, hooked on the unpredictable and intense," who tend to be "highly creative, outside-the-box thinkers, leaders in the arts, sports, business, science and politics". The gene is culturally significant and does in fact vary between racial populations. Its incidence is as high as forty percent in North American Indians. Ten percent of white Europeans and North Americans possess it. In China it is virtually nonexistent.[20]

Liberal geneticists are adamant in their assertion that hybridization is beneficial. Apart from hybrid vigor and reduction in the chance of deleterious homozygous combinations that hybridization offers, our interest is in the number of gifted people within a population. Let us now reduce the incidence of s in the native population from 0.60 to 0.06, as in Table 2. The frequency of aptitude in the hybrid population then becomes 2.9 people per 1000, *higher* than that of either native or migrant population, being an increase over the 1.9 gifted people per 1000 that had occurred in the native population, and the 1.7 per 1000 of the migrant population. That is, if each population of original, migrant and hybrid consisted of 10 million people, the original could give birth to 19,000 talented individuals, the migrant to 17,000, but a uniform mixture consisting of 20% migrant could give birth to 29,000: an increase over the unmixed populations. We now have an explanation for some prominent nations being the product of racial fusion.

Table 2:

Pop.	r	q	2qr	s	t	2st	2qr x 2st
Nat.	0.4	0.1	0.08	0.06	0.2	0.024	0.0019
Mig.	0.07	0.1	0.014	0.30	0.2	0.120	0.0017
Hyb.	0.334	0.1	0.0668	0.108	0.2	0.0432	0.0029

From a cursory examination of these tables we might argue either the racialist or liberal view, but to be noted in case 2 is that the beneficial results obtained from racial fusion are of a fortunate and limited mélange, where the mix is only beneficial up to s = 0.15 in the native population; beyond that a decline in the incidence of population talent occurs with mixture, shown in case 1. We cannot conclude, therefore, that mixture per se is beneficial, as the liberal would have us believe. The lesson is that if we have an *already successful* population, foreign mixture will probably diminish its incidence of genius and general caliber. In that case mass miscegenation is a genetic expression of entropic regression.

<u>Derivation of Table Frequencies</u>:

Given frequency of r in native population: 0.4; in migrant: 0.07. Let M = number of migrants, N = number of natives, then mixed population = M + N. Number of migrants with required gene = 0.07M; number of natives with required gene = 0.4N. Number of people with required gene in mixed population = 0.07M + 0.4N. Percent of mixed population with required gene:

$$r_2 = (0.07M + 0.04N)/(M + N)$$
M = 20% of mix, i.e., M = 0.2(M + N); N = 80% of mix, i.e., N = 0.8(M + N). Therefore:
$$r_2 = ((0.07)(0.2)(M + N) + (0.4)(0.8)(M + N))/(M + N)$$
$$= (0.07)(0.2) + (0.4)(0.8)$$
$$= 0.334$$

q was the same in both populations (0.1), therefore q_2 = 0.1. There will be a variety of other genes to occupy the required position on the chromosome, and we can give the sum of these other genes frequency p. Both males and females in the population will carry the genes equally, so by combining, the frequencies of all combinations in each generation will be:

$$(p + q + r)^2 = p^2 + 2pq + 2pr + q^2 + 2qr + r^2$$

It is the term 2qr that gives the proportion of individuals for the talent sought. By using given values, r = 0.4 and q = 0.1: 2qr = 2(0.1)(0.4) = 0.08. In hybrid population: $2q(r_2)$ = 2(0.1)(0.334) = 0.0668. With the migrants also differing from the native population in the frequencies s and t of other genes required for the talent, the frequency s_2 for the mixed population can be calculated the same way as r_2, and 2st found the same way as was found 2qr. Since the gene pairs qr and st are independent, the frequency of occurring together is 2qr x 2st.

These examples are based solely on numbers and do not depend on the *manner* that genes combine, whether first by meiosis or drawn from a hat. The reader, therefore, is not dependent on expertise for an evaluation of the thesis.

Appendix B

Historical Parallels:

We traditionally understand the range of human activity over the millennia to have been 'linear,' meaning that events have proceeded causationally from ancient times to the present, and that we of the modern world are in some degree necessarily influenced by what has gone before us. Associated with this understanding is the notion that the modern age, since it is the inheritor from past ages, must be superior to past ages in knowledge, enlightenment from superstition, personal freedom and material affluence. Undoubtedly there is some justification for this view, but to one thoroughly indoctrinated in it out of ignorance of the past, there come gasps of wonderment when he/she learns of ancient achievements. A list of just Hellenic accomplishment would include the application of levers, cranks, screws and cogwheels in ancient Greek industries, popular entertainment by marionettes in automatic theatres, war machines operated by air pressure, even automatic door openers, and washing machines that delivered water and mineral soap. In the sciences, the original discoverer that the Earth traveled around the sun was Aristarchus, 1800 years before Copernicus. The Earth, known to be a sphere, had its diameter estimated by Eratosthenes, who erred only by eighty kilometers. Anaxomandes discussed the evolution of life from lower forms, long before Charles Darwin, and Democritus speculated upon the atomic nature of matter. Schools of the Hellenistic Age were supported by the state, and at the Alexandrian Museum were lectures on astronomy, geography, physics, mathematics, botany, zoology, anatomy and medicine, where research by vivisection was done on animals. In their laboratories the Alexandrians discovered the nerves and learned that the brain controlled the limbs, a fact already known to the ancient Egyptians. In the earlier Age of Pericles, freedom of the intellect was championed by the Sophists, who openly rebuked the old religion and sought natural causes for earthly and celestial happenings. For males who were not slaves, the development of the individual reached its pinnacle in the Greek city-states, where democratic government complete with paid citizen juries was practiced. When the Romans came on the scene, companies were organized to build roads, bridges and aqueducts, which had shares daily sold to the public as in a modern stock exchange. Apartment living became common. The more fortunate merchants and bankers decorated their houses with the finest furniture, carpets and hangings, and had ornate bronze utensils, baths and sanitary conveniences. A more elaborate house would have tile pipes for conducting hot air to living rooms.

Time and again, in various geographical areas, remarkable achievements were realized in separate and distinct societies, societies that are lumped by the linear historian as the "ancient world". Accordingly, the "modern world" is the direct inheritor of what anomalous progress was made in the past grand age of ignorance, regardless of significant distinctions between concepts of the West and those of by-gone ages. Such distinctions involve our Western thought on space, for example, that would have seemed odd to an ancient Greek. Where we think of a straight line as "the shortest distance between two points," to the Greek mind it was the edge of a block. He/she was concerned with the immediate, sensual "here and now". Consequently, the most favored art form of ancient Greece was sculpture, whereas that of the West has been music. How different the basic outlook of these two societies, yet the Classical world is held to be the direct progenitor of the West. In like manner, the West differs significantly from India which cared nothing about time and never produced an historian. By contrast, ancient Egypt was completely concerned with time, and the subtle influence of time's unidirection was the essential motif of giant hallways, and statues that are meant to be viewed only from the front. In their psychological foundations ancient societies differed remarkably from each other, and from the West which in this respect must be considered an entity on its own.

Each civilization has had a unique life, and where there is life there is also death. To the superficially educated, the destruction of a great civilization comes with it being overrun by barbaric hordes, with, presumably, the example of Rome in mind, or through war that brought an end to the Aztec and Carthaginian empires, and which is especially easy to believe in today's age of atomic weapons. This popular view, of course, contains a grain of fact, but is not the kernel of truth, as any informed historian would readily agree with Toynbee's comment that of twenty-one occasions where civilization has been established, nineteen societies perished, not because of conquest but because of evaporation of substance from within. In other words, where a civilization has been erased from the world we should first look for evidence of decline inside its structure, for this is the enigma: the great societies of the past, like living organisms, have shown cultural deterioration on their own, when their institutions became spiritless, formalized, hierarchical, ruthless shells, which less sophisticated but more vigorous peoples did us the service of ending.

Thus we come to a new realization, that not only did

21 This historical vision follows the presentation of Amaury de Riencourt's "The Coming Caesars".

each past civilization possess a character unique to itself alone, after a period of strength and growth each experienced, on its own, internal debilitation and death. Knowing this, the pattern of history loses its 'linearity' and takes the appearance of cycles; which automatically leads us to ask about the West. Is it, too, subject to the same prospect of internal decay? The 'linear' view is not paramount for no reason. In it we can take comfort, for regardless of what conditions may be like at present we can look forward to an ever improving future. There is nothing more certain than progress; history proves it. Our optimism and confidence are shaken the moment we perceive that modern civilization might contain the same mortality of ancient societies, whose skeletons today dot our global landscape.

What evidence, then, do we have that our Western world is no different from past worlds in the sense that it possesses a life destiny, that like them it is subject to birth and decay, and must obey biological laws? To answer, we must explore world history on a holistic basis and see if parallels do exist between the various civilizations, named by historian, Oswald Spengler, *high cultures*, i.e., Sumerian, Egyptian, Mycenaean, Chinese, Indian, Mexican, Andean, Classical, Levantine, Russian and Western. The exercise will have more than academic importance since our perceptions have an obvious influence on the decisions we make. Political policies, in particular, will be different if a problem at hand is viewed inevitable and of long term seriousness rather than a temporary aberration, and also modern social trends might be better evaluated in the knowledge that "there is nothing new under the sun". In the words of George Santayana, "Those who cannot remember the past are condemned to repeat it."

The most remarkable parallel that can be drawn is between the Classical world and the Western,[21] for reasons that both developed around large bodies of water, the Mediterranean in the case of Greece and Rome, the Atlantic in the case of Europe and America, and both "high cultures" were originated by essentially the same race. Both began as the product of fusion, when barbaric invaders overran a more ancient and decadent society: the Dorian invasions in Greece over the remains of Mycenae, the Germanic invasions in Europe over the Roman Empire. Such invasions of vigorous barbarians over stagnated societies appear to be an encouraging factor in the birth of new dynamism, as occurred also with the Chow invasions of China and the Aryan invasion of India.

After the barbaric invasion a feudal system developed in Greece, headed by Homeric lords, just as Europe was ruled by feudal barons. Egypt's Pharonic Old Kingdom, the Chow era in China ruled by Chow princes, and Vedic India dominated by rajahs, represented the same feudal ages in those respective high cultures. Society has a hierarchical structure at this early stage, as well as always being intensely religious. So come eras when pyramids, temples and cathedrals are built, when religious thought is deep and religious "truth" is unquestioned.

Cities grew with the beginning of a commercial class and demise of the feudal order, while feudal territories merged into states. In China this maturation took place during the Spring and Autumn era, in India at the close of the Vedic era, in Egypt at the time of the fifth dynasty. The Mayan cities of Tikal, Copan, Naranjo and Piedras Negras flourished, as did Pachacamac, Chimu, Nazca and Tiahuanaco of the Andean Civilization. These are periods of unique perceptions and consequently of creativity in the arts and pure sciences, when people see the universe through new eyes and set out to explore for its own delight. New styles, concepts, innovations and techniques originated that formed the cultural basis of the different "high cultures," e.g., the Doric style of Greek architecture, the Gothic of the European. Such early stages are periods of original thought and creativity, of prototype as opposed to stereotype, and the essential soul of each "high culture" molds those creative expressions, even in the formation of the state. As the Greeks were concerned with the immediate, their concept of nationhood was limited to the city-state, that could be seen round about, whereas to the soaring Gothic spirit the nation could have a spacious extent. The Greeks spread commercial colonies throughout the Mediterranean just as European colonies later spread around the globe. Most notable of the Greek colonies was Syracuse, with opulence not unlike that of colonial Latin America.

The erosion of the feudal order is accompanied by reformation in religion and denouncement by religious leaders of the old social structure. Apollo was the god of Greece's Olympic faith, a god of poetry that symbolized harmony and beauty, whose prevalence became replaced in the seventh century BC by Dionysus, the god of the Orphic-Pythagorean social reformists. In like manner, Egypt's Heliopolitan clergy attempted to destroy the goddess Isis and replace her worship with that of the original sun-god, Ra, Buddha attacked Brahmanism with its caste privileges, and Islam was a religious revolution that eliminated much of Near Eastern art, to become the religion of traders and merchants. Similarly, Protestantism attacked Europe's Catholic faith, discarded religion as inspiration for the arts and became the pragmatic religion of dynamic capitalism.

With reformation, philosophical thought distanced itself from religion. Rationalism became a necessary adjunct to scientific inquiry, and 'free thinking' was the gentlemanly standard. The Goethes, Kants, utilitarians and empiricists of the West, the Sophists and Epicureans of ancient Greece, the Chinese schools of Mo Ti, Tzu Ssu, Mencius and Shang Yang, of the Indian Lokayata and Paribbajadas, and the rationalism of the Islamic Mu'tazila, were all expressions of an "Age of Reason" in their respective "high cultures".

Kings fell and new forms of more egalitarian government arose. The nation concept became more powerful and both Greece and Europe, bursting with internal energy, put their stamp on the known world with the conquests of older civilizations. Thus Alexander conquered Persia and Egypt just as later Europeans subjected India and China. The Greek cities even experienced an "industrial revolution," highlighted by enterprising Corinth. An age of unlimited optimism, peace and opulence ensued, known as the Hellenistic Era of the Classical world, the Victorian Era of the Western. By this time art had passed its last stage of genuine cultural expression, with the change from Doric to Ionian, from Gothic to Baroque. Pure culture became solidified and secondary to practical undertakings, collecting and cataloguing; scientific inquiry became the servant of medicine and engineering, art in the employ of commerce and luxury. Confidence was supreme and culminated with such constructions as the Titanic, the "unsinkable" ship.

But political and social upheavals mark the end of this purely cultural stage of great societies. All "high cultures" have experienced a period of fratricidal *world wars*: the Peloponnesian Wars of Greece; the period of Warring States in China; in India when the states of Kosala, Avanti, Vidha and Licchavi clashed; the wars of Sumeria that ravaged Ur, Uruk, Nippur, Eridu and Lagash; the destruction of the Mayan world with the conflicts between Uxmal, Mayapan and Chacmultun; the rise of the revolutionary Khurramiyya and Muhammira of the Near East; and, of course, the First and Second world wars of the West. This period may have associated with it a people closer to their barbaric roots who feel biologically superior to the effete populations of the older states. Thus the militaristic Macedonians entered Greek history as did the Prussians in Europe, as well as the Toltecs of Mexico whose stark architecture and fierce art supplanted the more ornate of the Mayas.

These periods of convulsion indicate a metamorphosis in the life of high cultures when genuine creativity has passed and the pure thought of by-gone ages is utilized for pragmatic works. Diffusion of ideas, art forms and patterns of social behavior from the centre of a civilized area is slower than the diffusion of material goods such as tools, weapons, vehicles, etc. The result is often stronger states at the edges of a civilized area than in the centre, because the centre is hampered by vested interests in the employment of its own innovations and because it devotes a larger part of its energy to nonmaterial culture. Inevitably, then, on the margins of a high culture are states predestined to swallow their worlds, which usually, in addition to their material advantages, have established beforehand the necessary psychological and social patterns. Thus it was with Rome, a state on the outskirts of Greek culture that eventually dominated Classical Civilization. It was little different with Chin, the state that conquered the whole of China, and of Persia that conquered the Sumerian world, or of the Turks in the Near East. The Aztec Empire, if not destroyed, would have embraced Mixtecs, Toltecs and Maya, just as the empire of the Incas conquered the Huari and Tiahuanaco peoples of the Andes.

Such world empires are efficient, pragmatic, legalistic and egalitarian. The achievements of Rome were not those of philosophy and art; rather they were of engineering, in the construction of aqueducts and highways, and of Roman law,

22 Gibbon: "The Decline and Fall of the Roman Empire," vol. 1, p. 49

which in that age of the 'common man' could postulate: "Better that a guilty man go free than an innocent man be convicted". Then as now a person was innocent until proven guilty. Women gained near equality with men, and could be more influential in society than was ever possible in ancient Greece. The practice of freeing slaves grew and laws protected the enslaved. The Roman Empire offered security from pirates and war, and produced an age of unrivalled prosperity upon every land, where roads, bridges, aqueducts, public baths, amphitheatres, constructed sewers, porticos, triumphal arches and grain elevators could be found. Eighty thousand kilometers of road crossed the civilized world, and lighthouses circled the Mediterranean that was speckled with ships carrying huge quantities of goods in regular shipping lanes. The empire was a free trading zone that stretched across the known world. "Pax Romana" became a byword. Exploitive imperialism became a practice of the past. Political authority did not require that one be born a Roman, not even the position of emperor: Trajan was a Spaniard, Severus an African, Diocletian and Constantine were Illyrians. Cities grew cosmopolitan, every free man of the Mediterranean world was granted Roman citizenship in 212 AD, and the government of Rome came to be a world government, ruling for the benefit of all peoples who were extended the same protection of justice, law and order.

> But the obedience of the Roman world was uniform, voluntary and permanent. The vanquished nations blended into one great people, resigned the hope, nay even the wish, of resuming their independence, and scarcely considered their own existence as distinct from Rome.[22]

Psychologically and sociologically the Roman era was little different from the present American. At that time, sensing a loss from former Greek predominance, intellects condemned the leveling Romanization of the world just as Americanization is frowned upon by many today. And, to complete the picture, the East, represented by Parthians and Jews, was as hostile to Rome as communist Russia to the United States. The world then was also divided between East and West. The former empire of Alexander in Asia was forever lost to the Romans, and that area, later to hold the Levantine "high culture," was a constant source of trouble. Alexander the Great imposed Greek culture upon unwilling peoples, which was as artificially rooted among them as the Europeanization of Peter the Great among resentful mujiks and clergy. The result was, when the opportunity was seized by the eastern nations to reclaim their own destinies, they became implacable enemies of those powers, Rome and America, that inherited the mantle from Greece and Europe.

The similarity between Roman and American characters was evident from their beginnings. Like the Puritans, the early Romans despised flippancy, instability and anything trifling. They had a sense of responsibility, earnestness and discipline. They reveled in hard work and had simple tastes. In contrast to the early Greek outlook such moral qualities do not suggest imagination or sense of beauty, but it is with such austere qualities that all world empires are begun, and with their loss is associated the downhill slide of the entire civilization. The pursuit of wealth, displayed in their dress, table, houses and furniture, and sensual gratification, became the standards by which Roman life was measured. Great villas arose, supported by slave worked plantations that could undercut the price of grain produced by independent farmers, resulting in the shrinkage of that sturdy class from which Rome, in earlier times, had drawn her armies. Since the country market for manufactured goods was drastically reduced, city industries could no longer dispose of their products and rapidly declined, their unemployed becoming a state burden. Cities enlarged, Rome itself containing one million inhabitants, and drained the countryside of wealth. Rome was filled with a shiftless mass that lived on state doles of meat and grain, that was content with the entertainment of bloody spectacles. Old Roman temples became disused, while imported gods and religions gained popularity. Lack of interest in public affairs increased, formerly responsible citizens turned indifferent. Celibacy and divorce became common, forcing Augustus to pass laws favoring marriage, yet sterility was sought and the Romans as a race disappeared from history.

Much the same picture is presented in every high culture after the establishment of its world empire. Conflicts and crises increase the need for a strong executive, resulting in the growth of the plebian power that eventually assumes total control. Julius Caesar merely fulfilled an inevitable trend, that was likewise fulfilled by Shih Hwangti of China, by Chandragupta of India, by Thutmose III of Egypt, and is today exemplified by growth of the American Presidency, an office that originally was considered little more than that of a Senator. The ensuing periods of decline are ages of giant cities filled with effeminized masses and the "high culture" surrendering to a mediocre mass of fellahin. From then on there are no grand exploits, one decade is the same as any other, and history becomes the chronology of world dicta- tors. The scene is then set for new waves of barbarians to conquer and create anew. The cycle is complete.

Appendix C

Christianity Examined:

And there is salvation through no one else; for there is no other name under heaven given among men by which we must be saved. (Acts 4: 12)

From quotations like the above, the Christian has been led for centuries to believe that his/her faith is unique, the one true light given for mankind's salvation, and that all non-Christian religions are the purest folly. To the Christian, knowledge of God was the gift of Abraham and the Jewish prophets to a fallen world, which culminated in the teachings of a one-and-only Savior who died so we might live eternally in paradise. Armed with the arrogance of the ideologue and confident of doing "God's work," the Christian has ventured into the outer darkness of the world's pagan religions with all the fervor and missionary zeal which only the righteous can muster, for to such believers all else is depravity and devil-worship. It should be of no little concern to the believing Christian, then, to find that the teachings of Christ are not particular to Christianity, and that the development of his/her faith can be traced to the very paganism he/she condemns. Far from being a unique religion, Christianity was merely the last and most successful of numerous god-man savior cults to appear in the Mediterranean world,

---

23 All historical accounts are derived from *The Story of Christian Origins,* by Martin A. Larson, c. 1977, Joseph J Binns/New Republic Book.

which had the ground work for its acceptance prepared by thousands of years of very similar *mysteries*. By accepting Christianity the pagans of that time were not undergoing a radical transformation of belief habits; on the contrary, those beliefs had been evolving for millennia and were common throughout the area. To this day, regardless of all the zealots, missions, Crusades and colonial conquests, Christianity remains predominantly Western; even the Jews rejected it. Under colonial rule it never became a force in India, not to mention China and Japan regardless of earnest attempts. In areas where Christianity was firmly planted outside European culture, this was done by the Spanish sword, or it has survived meaningfully by incorporating and tolerating the local beliefs which continue side-by-side with the Church to this day. Why it became the religion of the West is owing to the specific development of religion in the West. That development was pagan, and has been clearly outlined by theological historians.

The roots of Christianity go back over five thousand years,[23] not to the land of the "Chaldean Ur" (Gen. 11: 31), but to Egypt, when invaders from Mesopotamia overran that country and imposed the worship of Osiris, a religion which over the centuries absorbed the attributes associated with the indigenous gods. According to that myth, Osiris was a benevolent king of Egypt killed by his evil brother, Set, represented by a serpent, but was resurrected by his wife and sister, Isis. By breathing into his nostrils Isis brought Osiris to eternal life, whereby he went to rule the land of immortals and judge the dead. After a war with the evil Set, Horus, the son of Isis, crushed the serpent's head and the gods condemned Set to destruction by fire. Just as Isis and Horus became the prototypes for Madonna and Child, Osiris was the "first fruits of them that slept" to the Egyptians. Everyone lived and toiled in hope of obtaining the same immortality as their god. Upon death, provided one's physical body were preserved, it was believed the person who had lived a moral life, who had not committed robbery, violence, murder, adultery, sodomy, falsehood, who was not guilty of irreverence, insolence, deceit or causing an unjust increase in wealth, entered paradise to live forever, or if unworthy his heart and soul were devoured and his body burned in the Lake of Fire. But even if he were "clean of mouth and hand" he could not enter paradise without the mercy of Osiris at judgment.

Integral to the Egyptian belief in immortality was eating bread that represented the flesh of Osiris, and drinking barley ale to represent his blood. Without partaking in this Eucharist no one could achieve eternal life. This Osirian sacrament had its origin in cannibalism practiced by the original inhabitants of the Nile valley, and became refined under the conquering invaders who substituted wheat and beer for actual flesh. Savages around the world commonly believe that the qualities of people eaten become their own, and this notion was transplanted into the Osiris doctrine, where the quality sought was the immortality of the god-man. Subsequently, Osiris came to be associated with a divine seed to give life to humanity, and emotional passion plays were enacted depicting the life, death and resurrection of the god-man.

The influences of Egyptian civilization were not confined to Egypt; they spread widely along trade routes and the same themes of Osiris-worship recurred throughout the ancient world, under the god-heads of Bromius, Sabazius, Attis, Adonis, Zalmoxis, Corybas and Serapis. Prevalent everywhere was belief in a god-man dying to give salvation, usually associated with a sacrament.

The cult of Dionysus was originally introduced into

Greece from Egypt by a priest named Melampus, then again from Thrace around 1200 B.C. Dionysus was the son of Zeus and human Semele, a Savior born from the union of god and mortal; the similarity to Christ as "the Son of God" born from the human Mary is to be noted. His veneration among barbarians was originally associated with eating raw flesh, either of a cow or child, in order that his worshippers become immortal "Bacchoi". Dionysus's worshippers mourned his death with savage pain, while his resurrection was celebrated with ecstatic orgies. The cult was phallic. Eventually it was reformed by Orphism, the first reform being the substitution of bread and wine for flesh as a sacrament. Orphism taught original sin, judgment after death, reward and punishment in an afterlife, and the notion of Dionysus as a Savior who died for mankind.

A popular cult of the ancient Mediterranean, found from Asian Phrygia to Spain, and which possibly dated as far back as 1800 B.C., was that of Attis and his mother Cybele: an amalgam of Osiris-worship with Semitic religion. This cult did not have a sacrament but offered immortality and escape from sin through castration and repudiation of sex, which was not a drastic innovation since the Osirian priests were celibates. In addition to forsaking erotic desire, devotees whipped, beat, slashed and otherwise mutilated themselves. In Phrygia, the effigy of Attis during the annual festival of Cybele was impaled upon the trunk of a pine tree and carried into the temple. After two days of frenzied, demented public mourning and sacrifice of virility, priests removed the effigy and laid it in a tomb. The next day, March 25th, the tomb was opened and found to be empty, indicating that the god, Attis, had been resurrected to eternal life. The cult also had a blood baptism, using the blood of a bull to give the inductee a symbolic rebirth.

Thus it is evident that the soteriology of Christianity, the belief in a god-man dying to give his followers eternal life, did not originate with Jesus Christ. In every case where it was found it preceded Christianity, meaning that this most sacred belief of Christian dogma was inherited, and that inheritance is pagan. But this is only concerning Christ as the Savior, and belief in immortality. There is much more to Christianity, which brings us to ancient Iran.

About the year 600 BC the prophet Zoroaster, as his religion told, was born of a virgin mother. At the age of thirty, after undergoing a sacred water baptism and being tempted by the devil with promises of power and magnificence, he began to preach his doctrine of heaven, hell and purgatory, cosmic dualism and apocalyptic renovation of the world. In his theology the universe was divided between the rule of Ahuramazda, the God of light and virtue, associated with a holy spirit named Pure Wind, and that of Ahriman, the god of darkness and evil, with his demons. Ahuramazda was the creator of everything good and beneficial to man, Ahriman the creator of everything harmful. Time was divided into various periods represented by gold, silver, brass, copper, iron and tin, suggesting successive degeneration. The end of the tenth millennium would be wrought with deception, hate, apostasy, lack of affection, and be afflicted with earthquakes and wars. At the end of this millennium the messiah, Hushedar, also born of a virgin, would re-establish the religion of Ahuramazda with the conversion of one third of humanity. Another messiah at the end of the eleventh millennium would have two thirds of humanity worshipping in the good religion, and again after the twelfth millennium the great Saoshyant would establish the universal Kingdom of Righteousness. Before that happened, however, Ahriman would mobilize his forces for an all out war. The archfiend,

Azi-Dahak, would be released from the infernal pit to slay one third of mankind, cattle and sheep, and the earth would run with rivers of blood (compare with Revelation 8: 7,9,11 and 9: 15). After the victory of Saoshyant, everyone, good and bad, would be resurrected to face judgment (see Revelation 20: 12,13,14), when the wicked would be parted from the virtuous and sent into hell for purification. Finally, hell, Ahriman and all his demons would be destroyed forever.

Shortly before 500 BC these two belief systems, the savior cults and Zoroastrianism, came together. The first synthesis was the work of a universal genius, known today as a geometrician, but a man who was also an astronomer, philosopher, social revolutionary and theologian: Pythagoras. The Pythagoreans, as we may call his followers, were definitely monotheistic, in contradiction to Christian belief that worship of a single God was not practiced by gentiles before Christianity. The God of the Pythagoreans was a universal, spiritual force of whom any representation in the form of pictures or statues was forbidden. Originally a social as well as a religious movement, the Pythagoreans became quite powerful, but aroused hostility because of their communistic brotherhoods. The hostility led to massacres, one at Croton in 510 BC, another in southern Italy in 450 BC. The movement was eventually destroyed politically because its members were pacifists who refused to protect themselves, and it became purely religious.

Pythagoras traveled in Egypt, Chaldea and India, and it was during these travels that he learned elements of Zoroastrianism and Brahmanism, especially concerning doctrines of heaven and hell. It was he who introduced these notions into the Occident. Other beliefs of the Pythagoreans included repudiation of all passion, especially the sexual, with renouncement of the family and property. They practiced baptismal purification with water, forbade oaths, had a Eucharist of bread and wine, used white garments, practiced healing and non-violence, believed in cosmic dualism with worship of the sacrificed Orphean god-man, and believed that people were predestined to be either of the Elect or Reprobate; they despised earthly riches, were vegetarians, celibates and fervent missionaries.

The second synthesis occurred in Palestine, where further elements of Zoroastrianism merged with Pythagoreanism, beginning with a party of religious enthusiasts called "Hasidim". The Hasidim remodelled the Jewish Messiah on the Zoroastrian Saoshyant, and incorporated beliefs of heaven, hell, immortality, resurrection and final judgment into the original Judaism. The Hasidim then split into Pharisees and Essenes, the Pharisees externalizing religion into an elaborate formalism, the Essenes considering themselves the Elect amid apocalyptic saints who would rule after Judgment Day. Until shortly before 100 BC the Essenes were essentially Zoroastrian Judaists, but then a leader arose among them called the "Teacher of Righteousness" who gave them the discipline and mysteries of Pythagoras. The Essenes then observed holy days different from the orthodox and ignored the temple worship, took no oath, were pacifists, rejected marriage, taught the immortality of souls, practiced baptism and communism, and had a Eucharist. Ample record of their beliefs and practices has been left in the Dead Sea Scrolls, composed between 170 BC and 60 BC, and also in the writings of Josephus and Philo of Alexandria, the latter himself an Essene. Upon the arrest, trial and death of their "Teacher of Righteousness" the Essenes believed he would return surrounded by angels to set up the Kingdom of Heaven on Earth, after performing the Last Judgment and sending all the worldly to a flaming hell. They identified him with the "Lamb of God" and sinless Savior of their writings who would die for ungodly men, and believed his execution brought divine retribution upon the Jews - all before the Christian era. By 25 AD the Essene messiah had failed to return, but the country was rife with expectation just before the ministry of Jesus Christ. Yet all the ingredients of Christianity have still not been listed. The remainder returns us to 557 BC.

Gautama Buddha, after pre-existing as a heavenly spirit, was born of Queen Maya who ascended into heaven upon his birth. As the legend goes, angels sang when he was born and it was prophesied that he would rule the world. After achieving enlightenment he was tempted by the god of this world with worldly power and sensualism to not begin preaching. His doctrine involved the Kingdom of Righteousness that was to be established on Earth as a physical reality, he taught in parables that included one of the Prodigal Son, and performed miracles.

India at that time was a land of grotesque social injustice. The ruling caste of priest-kings, the Brahmans, had appropriated to themselves most privileges and wealth, made all religious and civil decisions and all codes of law, and monopolized learning. At the base of their society were the Sudras and outcasts who performed all work and were virtual slaves, whose main purpose in life was to serve the higher castes. The worst punishment that could be inflicted on a Brahman was banishment, whereas if a Sudra so much as listened to a Veda being recited he had molten metal poured into his ears; he could be mutilated for the most minor infringements against Brahmans and whipped to death on any pretext. Not only did the Brahmans terrorize in this world they also prescribed the most graphic torments in twenty-three hells for anyone expressing independence from their control. Violent revolt against such a priest state was impossible; the method adopted derived from Brahmanic asceticism. The masses went on strike; no amount of beating or flogging could make them pick up their tools, for, led by the teachings of Gainism and Buddhism, they renounced this world and the worldly Brahmans. The doctrine of hell was turned around, to become reserved for those whose reward was in this life. In the new asceticism all were equally welcome: Sudras, outcasts, harlots, thieves and murderers. Buddhism represented the world's first universal brotherhood of the oppressed and poor. Along with it came renunciation of gold, cattle, land, comfort, and of family and sex that lead to toil. Property became a moral contaminant that could be purged only by giving to the poor. Buddhism taught pacifism and nonviolence, the return of love for hate, kindness for abuse, that one should harbor no anger or resentment, and that sin is in the desire more than the act. It sought only conversion, not control of society, and had no barriers to membership or rules against divulging doctrine. Buddhist missionaries journeyed world wide, to Greece, Egypt, Persia and Asia Minor, the latter teeming with proselytizers by the first century.

Thus by the time of Christ all the ingredients of Christianity were in place. Due to these similarities with established doctrines, many scholars have wondered if Jesus Christ was an actual historical figure. Their skepticism was not moderated by notable authors of the time failing to mention his existence. Justus of Tiberias was a native of Galilee who lived immediately after the death of Jesus, but says nothing about his life. Josephus has one passage but it is considered a forgery because Christians of the first two centuries made no mention of it, and it was written by a Christian whereas Josephus was a Pharisee. He does mention John, the brother of Jesus, however, and the existence of

Christ is confirmed by Tacitus' Annals 15: 44. But these are scanty reports for a man whose birth caused every male child under two years old in Bethlehem to be murdered by the wicked King Herod (Matt. 2: 16), of which there is no other report, nor was King Herod even alive when this deed supposedly happened; whose birth was heralded by a star that wise men in the East could recognize and follow (Matt. 2: 2); whose fame spread over the country (Luke 4: 14); whose death caused the earth to shake, rocks to split, temple veil to tear in two, and even dead saints to be raised who were later seen in Jerusalem (Matt. 27: 51-53).

The obvious discrepancies that appear between the Four Gospels also do not help to make the story believable. Christ's genealogies of Matthew and Luke do not agree, give a different number of generations, and both trace his lineage through Joseph although Christ was not supposed to be Joseph's flesh and blood. In Matthew, Jesus is born in a house before the death of Herod, wise men visited him, and the family fled to Egypt. In Luke, Jesus is born in a stable during the governorship of Cyrenius, was visited by shepherds and there is no journey to Egypt. After the crucifixion, the Matthew account is of two women, Mary Magdalene and another Mary, discovering the empty tomb, Jesus meets them on their way to tell the disciples and orders that the disciples go to Galilee, and the ascension is from a mountain in Galilee. In Mark, three women, the two Marys and Salome, find a young man in the tomb who commands them to tell the disciples to go to Galilee, and the ascension is from a room. According to Luke, two women see two men at the tomb who inform them of the resurrection, Jesus appears to the disciples at a meeting and tells them to wait in Jerusalem, and the ascension is from Gethany. In John it is Mary Magdalene alone who discovers the empty tomb, Jesus speaks to her outside the tomb, and the ascension is from the Sea of Galilee.

That there should be lack of agreement between the Gospels is to be expected, because all were written years after the events, Mark between 60 and 67 AD, John not before 120 AD, all were originally written in Greek, and none by eye witnesses. And during this hiatus there was ample opportunity for the original story, whatever it was, to be elaborately worked upon by minds already steeped in the myths and fables of existing creeds. The Immaculate Conception is undoubtedly such an addition. One of the earliest Christian sects was that of the Ebionites, who were Christian Jews. Their writings do not mention a Virgin Birth. Their rendition of Luke 3: 22 was: "Thou art my beloved Son, in thee I am well pleased. *This day have I begotten thee.*" (emphasis added). To the Ebionites, Christ was the Son of God only in a spiritual sense, and he became that Son at baptism. This explains why Christ's genealogy is given through Joseph. The latter phrase of the quotation was removed from the Christian Bible after 400 AD. The reason is clear: to agree with the concept of Immaculate Conception and make Christianity more palatable to the heathen, who were used to their saviors being of divine stuff.

The impractical and at times immoral teachings of Christianity have already been commented on in *Cosmos Theology* (page 45). Compared to the Old Testament the change in morality of those teachings is striking. In place of the admonition against property, Isaiah unabashedly proclaims to the Jews: "..the wealth of the nations shall come to you." (Isaiah 60: 5); "You shall drink the milk of the nations and drain the wealth of kings;" (Isaiah 60: 16); "You shall partake of the wealth of the nations, and with their riches you shall become famous." (Isaiah 61: 6). Instead of loving one's enemies, the order from Moses to prevent "contamination" when taking the Promised Land is: "But in cities in the area which the Lord your God is giving you, you shall not keep alive one that has breath; you must wipe them out completely..." (Deut. 20: 16,17). Accounts abound of King David slaying Israel's enemies in war: "He struck down Moab; he made them lie on the ground and measured them with a line, designating two parts for death,.." (II Samuel 8: 2). A leader who did that today would be considered a war criminal. "..David struck down 22,000 of the men of Syria.." (II Samuel 8: 5). After taking the city of Rabbah, King David enslaved the inhabitants: "..the people that were in (the city) he brought out and put to labor with saws and iron picks and axes, forcing them to keep working in the brickmolds." (II Samuel 12: 31). The offspring from King David's adultery with Bathsheba was the "wise" King Solomon, who, far from making himself a eunuch, had 700 official wives and 300 concubines (I Kings 11: 3). In Song of Solomon, chapter seven, we are given a lusty appraisal of the female anatomy: "Your rounded thighs are a jeweled chain...Your navel is as a rounded bowl...your belly as a heap of wheat...Your breasts are as two fawns..." etc. Judah, on the road to Timnath, saw a veiled woman whom he though was a harlot and requested: ".. 'Let me please come in to you!'.." (Genesis 38: 16) which he did for the price of a goat. Lest it be though that Judah was not one of God's favorites, we read in Revelation 7: 5, "Of the tribe of Judah twelve thousand were sealed," as the servants of God, and learn from Revelation 5: 5 that the only one worthy of opening the apocalyptic scroll was "..the Lion out of the tribe of Judah." Genesis 12 gives account of Abraham surrendering his wife (and half sister) to Pharaoh in Egypt, for which he was rewarded with "..flocks, herds, donkeys, male and female slaves, she-donkeys and mules." As if to prove that this behavior is fine with God, in chapter 20 he does the same with Abimelech, king of Gerar. Again he is handsomely rewarded. We have to ask what man of character would journey to a foreign country where he knew such virtual pimping of his wife would be necessary. Lot offered his two virgin daughters to a depraved multitude in the city of Sodom: "..let me bring them out to you, and you do with them as you like;" (Genesis 19: 8). We should not consider Lot's daughters chaste, however, for after getting him drunk in the mountains, to save his line: "..the two daughters of Lot conceived by their father." (Genesis 19: 36).

How can two opposite views on morality be presented between the covers of the same "inspired" book? If morality is absolute, being what God wants from us, an act is moral or immoral irrespective of time, place or performer, and if the men and women of the Bible were truly people of God, their behavior would have set shinning examples for all generations for all time. Must we not question the value of a book as a moral guide that presents such ambiguity?

As if the pagan origins of Christianity evident in the Bible were not enough, institutionalized Christianity has added beliefs and practices that have made the paganization of that religion virtually complete. We might think that nothing could be more Christian than the cross, until we learn that it is a modification of the Egyptian *ank*, or cross worn by Egyptian priests. Surely an emblem representing the instrument of torture and death of a religious founder is a strange symbol for that religion. The name "Easter" is reminiscent of Ishtar, the Mesopotamian goddess whose worship was associated with an egg and Lent of forty days. The concept of the Trinity was known in ancient Assyria, where it was represented by a triune emblem showing the head of an old man, a circle and the wings of a bird, portraying Father, Son and Spirit. Idol processions, relic worship, rosaries;

24 Rev. Alexander Hislop, *The Two Babylons.*

www.ingramcontent.com/pod-product-compliance
Lightning Source LLC
Chambersburg PA
CBHW052106090426
42741CB00009B/1702